The Information Society

The Information Society

as Post-Industrial Society

Yoneji Masuda

Institute for the Information Society
Tokyo Japan

First U.S. printing (1981) by:
World Future Society
4916 St. Elmo Avenue
Bethesda, MD 20814 ● U.S.A.

Book design and diagrams
by Gow Michiyoshi and Kazuaki Sinohara

Library of Congress Cataloging in Publication Data

Masuda, Yoneji
The Information Society

Includes index.
1. Information Science. 2. Technology-Social aspect.
3. Computerization. I. Title
DDC (Edition 19)   303.483   UDC   301.18:681.3.009

ISBN 0-930242-15-7

Printed in the United States of America

to you who believe in Mankind's wisdom, goodwill and future

Preface and Acknowledgements

Mankind is now entering a period of transformation from an industrial society to an information society, and my aim in this book is to attempt a prediction of its character and structure, and to present an overall view of what such a society would be.

When we look back over the development of human society, we see that human history has embraced three types of society: hunting, agricultural, and industrial. It is important to note that rapid innovations in *the system of societal technology* have usually become the axial forces that have brought about these societal transformations. Such a system of societal technology shows four fundamental characteristics:

1. Many different kinds of innovational technology come together to constitute one complex technological system.
2. These integrated systems of technology spread throughout society and gradually become established.
3. The result is a rapid expansion of a new type of productivity.
4. The development of this new type of productivity has societal impact sufficient to bring about the transformation to new societal forms of what had become traditional.

Hunting society proceeded from innovation in societal technology based on systems concerned with hunting. Similarly, the bases for societal transformation first to agricultural society and then to industrial society were innovations in systems of societal technology concerned with agriculture and industrial production. Man is now standing at the threshold of a period of innovation in a new societal technology based on the combination of computer and communications technology. This is a completely new type of societal technology, quite unlike any of the past. Its substance is information, which is invisible.

This new societal technology will bring about societal transformation in society which, in a double sense, is unprecedented.

First: the transformation of society is the result of innovations in societal technology, which, in the past, have always been concerned with physical productivity. Even these rapid expansions of physical productivity brought about a change from the feudalistic self-sustained economic system based on agricultural production to a freely competitive goods economy based on industrial production.

Second: the current innovation in societal technology, however, is not concerned with the productivity of material goods, but with information productivity, and for this reason can be expected to bring about fundamental changes in human values, in trends of thought, and in the political and economic structures of society. It will be necessary to boldly build a new paradigm which is free of traditional concepts if we are to offer the future image of this information society. This can be done by using the *historical analogy and pattern analysis* of past societies. Reducing the structure of *human* society into major components, such as values, trends of thought, innovational technology, the market, economic structure, political systems, I propose to present the pattern of a new concept of each of these components by which to construct an overall composition of the future information society. We are placing the major emphasis on a pattern analysis of industrial society, and the historical analogy that applies to the information society.

This book consists of two parts. Part I deals as concretely and factually as possible with the question of when and through what stages information society will be created. For this purpose, I discuss the Japanese plan for information society as a blueprint of information society drawn up in Japan, and its actual results, and touches on model experiments on information society presently being made in Canada and Sweden. Then I draw a picture of an overall composition of information society as opposed to industrial society, and make projections on the realization process of information society, while analyzing the developmental stages of actual computerization. Lastly, I make a prediction on when information society will be realized, by comparing the tempo of the motive power revolution and that of the computer revolution.

Part II concerns the author's theoretical and conceptual studies on information society. First, I discuss the essential nature of computer-communications technology, the basic characteristic features of the information epoch brought about by this technology, and its social and economic impact. From there I go on to the elements of my conceptual framework for the information society: globalism, time value, the goal principle, the information utility, a synergetic economic system, information democracy, participatory democracy, voluntary communities, and finally, a vision of Computopia.

This book is completely rewritten version, for English publication, of the book 'Information Economics', published by Sangyo Noritsu University press, and parts of the book have already been issued in abbreviated form as listed below.

'Societal Impact of Computerization - Application of the Pattern Model to Industrial Society,' Proceedings of the First International Future Research Conference, Kyoto, Japan, April, 1970.

'A New Development Stage of the Information Revolution,' Applications of Computer/Telecommunications Systems, OECD, November, 1972.

'Management of Information Technology for Developing Countries - Adaptation of Japanese Experience to Developing Countries,' Data Exchange, April, 1974, Diebold Europe.

'The Conceptual Framework of Information Economics' IEEE Transaction on Communications, Vol. Com-23, No. 10, October, 1975.

'Automated States vs. Computopia: Unavoidable Alternatives for the Information Era,' — The Next 25 Years, Crisis and Opportunity, World Future Society, 1975.

'Conceptual Structure of Information Economics,' Proceedings of the 3rd International Conference on Computer Communication, Toronto, Canada, August, 1976.

'A New Era of Global Information Utility,' Proceedings of Eurocomp 78, London, England, May, 1978.

'Future Perspectives for Information Utility,' Proceedings of the 4th International Conference on Computer Communication, Kyoto, Japan, September, 1978.

'Privacy in the Future Information Society,' Computer Networks, Special Issue, June, 1979.

It would be impossible for me full to express my deep and sincere appreciation to my mentors, family, friends and colleagues in various parts of the world, including Japan.

First of all, I would like to dedicate this book with deep veneration to the memory of the late Reverend Seiichi Yukawa, mentor of long standing, who invoked divine protection for me to complete the publication of this book, but died before it could see the light of day.

Then I would like to thank from the bottom of my heart my wife Fujie and my son Shigeru, always showing affection and deep understanding of my work.

I also would like to express my gratitude to Mr. Douglas Parkhill and Mr. Tomas Ohlin who provided me with valuable government data and made constructive suggestions.

Finally, I would like to thank Bernard Halliwell for his perseverance in the very difficult task of translating the Japanese manuscript into English. His monumental effort to understand the concepts and presentation of ideas in this book has made this English version possible.

I should also wish to make specific mention of the long collaboration of Atsushi Yamada who translated my many articles for the various international conferences. Mrs. Maria Radon's proof reading of the galley sheets is deeply appreciated and reflected her perseverance and understanding. The preparation of the English text and the typing of the MS for this book were the work of Andrew Hughes and his wife Tomoko, for which I would like to express my sincere appreciation. Their team work and the ideas of this book are epitomized on the title page of Part II written by Mr. Hughes.

The quotation on the title page of Part I is by courtesy of Dr. Herbert A. Simon. Fig. 1.1 by courtesy of the Japan Computer Usage. Development Institute, and Fig. 1.2, 1.3 by courtesy of the Living Visual Information System Development Association.

Tokyo, Japan
June 1980   Yoneji Masuda

Contents

PART ONE
EMERGENCE OF THE INFORMATION SOCIETY

In recorded history there have perhaps been three pulses of change powerful enough to alter Man in basic ways. The introduction of agriculture....The Industrial Revolution... (and) the revolution in information processing technology of the computer .... [1]

—Herbert A. Simon—

1
Emerging Information Society in Japan

One of the most interesting actions has occurred in Japan, where in 1972 a non-profit organization called the Japan Computer Usage Development Institute presented to the government 'The Plan for Information Society — A national goal toward the year 2000.'[2] This plan had been developed for presentation as a model plan for the realization of Japan's information society. It gives a picture of an information society that is desirable and can be realized by 1985. It also includes an integrated plan involving various projects for the construction of the blue-printed information society. I am very honored and consider myself fortunate to have been appointed project manager of this ambitious national plan.

Outline of the Plan for Information Society

The goal of the plan is the realization of *a society that brings about a general flourishing state of human intellectual creativity, instead of affluent material consumption.*[3]

If the goal of industrial society is represented by volume consumption of durable consumer goods or realization of heavy mass consumption centering around motorization, information society may be termed as a society with highly intellectual creativity where *people may draw future designs on an invisible canvas and pursue and realize individual lives worth living.*

The plan includes an 'Intermediate Impact Plan' that was to have required an investment of $3 million between 1972 and 1977, and a 'Long Term Basic Plan' that calls for an investment of $65 billion between 1972 and 1985.

A) Administration Data Bank ($300 million)
This project is aimed at controlling through distribution and concentration the administrative data compiled by government offices,

and offering services through batch disposal or on-line processing and disposal of these data as required by the government offices.

This would contribute to the formulation of administrative policy and become the major information supply source to universities and general enterprises.

The systems would be divided into:

a. Information retrieval of administrative data
b. Policy module and policy programme

The basic composition of the systems would be:

a. The nation's major statistical data collected over the past decade.
b. The preparation and use of many policy module units required to prepare a programme for formulation of policy.
Remarks: Example of policy module:
'Calculation of number of primary schools in each prefecture in 1980.'
   In this case, the estimated number of the population at primary school age, the standard number of classes, teachers, and other numerical data are combined into one unit.

B) Computopolis Plan ($1,169 million)

Computopolis is a 'computerized city' expected to be developed in the future information society.

In this project, experiments would be conducted on a model of the future information society to be built as a new town similar to the currently developed Tama new town. The core of urban computerization would consist of systems such as:

a. CATV
b. CVS (computer controlled vehicle system)
c. Automated supermarket
d. Regional health control
e. Regional cooling and heating system

CATV would not consist merely of multi-channel TV broadcasts by cable, but would involve inquiries from individual homes, constituting two-way information services, such as:

a. Local news
b. Shopping and leisure consultation

c. Emergency communication, such as fires
d. Medical and infant nursing consultation
e. Education

CVS is a transportation network in a new town, with automatically controlled passenger cars on rails, each designed to carry two persons. The automated supermarket would have no service personnel. It would supply fresh food and be equipped with automatic refrigeration warehouse, sample selling system, using magnetic cards, and would operate in direct contact with producers.

Local health control is a medical information system comprising disease prevention and health control. Individual medical records will be kept for all residents of the new town, with semi-annual health checks.

C) Regional Remote Control Medical System ($277 million)

A model experimental area may be designated, incorporating an overall medical project in accordance with the long term basic plan. Centering on local health control systems through a completely automated hospital, the system would incorporate remote control health care and emergency medical systems. A model area would have a population of about 100,000, and the automated hospital would comprise a total system involving office work, diagnosis, medical treatment and clinical studies.

A model experimental area may be designated, incorporating ME (medical engineering) equipment technology, and case history files would be combined and studied in such a laboratory. This model hospital would maintain contact with isolated islands and isolated regions and develop a standard model of a remote health care system through communication, physical tests and case history files. At the same time, traffic accidents occurring in the vicinity would be handled as an emergency aid medical system.

D) Computer-Oriented Education in an Experimental School District ($266 million)

An experimental school district would conduct computer oriented education in preschool, kindergarten, primary school, junior and senior high schools, centering around a university such as the education university. Details of the projects would be in accordance with the long term basic plan, including:

a. Rationalization of school office work
b. Individual education guidance system

c. Computer oriented education

d. Educational science research center

The combination of such projects would contribute to:

a. Solving problems on future computer oriented education

b. Measuring the educational effect of the intelligence network

c. Planning a standard education system

d. Developing a new individual education system

. In conducting this educational experiment, emphasis should be placed on objective and scientific data collection and analysis, taking into account the differences in results of the two educational systems, one being the computer-oriented, private-instruction, problem-solving type of educational system; and the other, the contemporary group uniform educational system. The introduction of computers into education will arouse school-teacher resistance, possibly a crucial point.

E) Pollution Prevention System over a Broad Region ($584 million)

This development is of an integrated pollution prevention system to be applied to polluted areas such as the Mizushima area. It would include both direct and indirect measuring, warning, and control systems, with a pollution information center in each polluted area, and a communication network linking the information center with sources of pollution.

The pollution involved would not be only effluent and gas emissions from factories, but also atmospheric pollution, oceans and rivers, and include garbage disposal. Polluting sources to be considered would be factories, buildings, automobiles, etc.; in fact, all facilities.

The prevention research center would develop the necessary pollution measuring equipment, pollution prevention technology, and waste disposal and processing technology. The essential cooperation of the general public would require the formation of a pollution prevention citizens' conference.

F) Think-Tank Center ($386 million)

In central Tokyo, a high rise building of the size of Kasumigaseki Building would be needed to accommodate all the nation's think-tanks, both governmental and private. Facilities for common use by the think-tanks would be equipped with computers, various models, programmes, library, discussion rooms, experiment facilities, etc. This center and the government's data bank, the scientific technology information center, and other data banks would operate on an online system. The facilities would be open to those think-tanks that may be formed temporarily for individual projects, which are important to foster.

A special education center corresponding to a graduate school would have to be established in this center for the education of corporate managers, specialists, and engineers. An education course that would enable participants to qualify for a Master's or even a Doctor's degree would be necessary.

Another facility would be a citizen's participation center. A model experiment in the nature of a people's political consensus reflection system would enable citizens to participate in group discussions and use policy model simulation for resolving social and economic problems.

G) Introduction of MIS in Small Enterprises ($127 million)

The modernization of small enterprises would be speeded up by the introduction of management information system.

For this purpose a small enterprise information center would embrace some 10,000 selected enterprises for business consultation, providing a monthly presentation of corporate management data.

Each enterprise would be equipped with terminal equipment connected with the center, and input and output of data by remote groups would be possible. Data and files for consultation between small and medium enterprises would be prepared at the center, and specialists would provide guidance, together with seminar facilities for managers and accountants of small companies.

H) Labour Re-Development Center ($179 million)

This center would be necesary for the retraining of middleaged and senior citizens, with a training capacity for some 1,000 people throughout the year. The training would not be merely instruction on technical matters for the purpose of re-employment, but for discovery and development of potential and latent personal faculties of each person, by checking career files and personality tests. Counselling and guidance would enable each individual to be guided in planning and developing faculties for oneself, thereby opening the way to further employment. The education and training would guide each person to initiate one's own social activities, and be intended to introduce aged persons to new jobs.

The system would be devised so the development of new employment opportunities will be possible by having a broad information

Fig. 1.1 The Plan for Information Society: A National Goal
toward the Year 2000

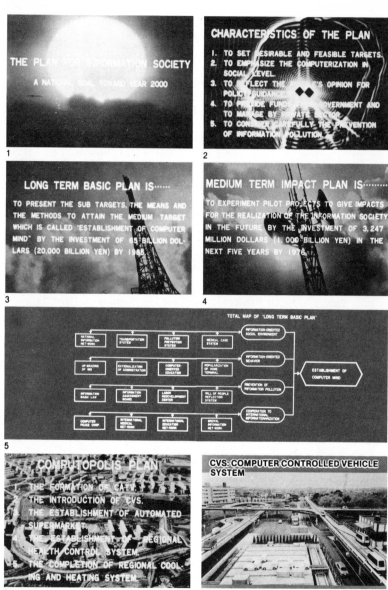

Source: By Courtesy of the Japan Computer Usage Development Institute

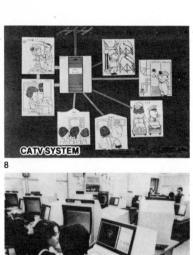

8 CATV SYSTEM

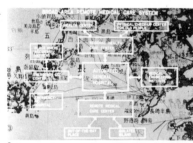

9

10 CAI: COMPUTER AIDED INSTRUCTION

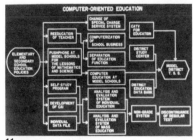

11

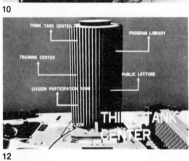

12

13

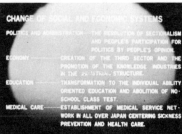

14

15

network of available resoures. Lodging facilities would be necessary in this labour center so that participants can begin a new social life through mutual communication.

I) Computer Peace Corp ($10 million)

A computer peace corp would be a powerful boost to reinforce economic aid to developing countries. A team, consisting of systems analysts, programmers, engineers and managers in the electronic computer field, could be organized.

International Opinion Poll on this Plan

An interesting aspect of this project is that a detailed national and international opinion poll[4] was taken on various key aspects of this plan. Five hundred and sixty persons were polled, 372 living in Japan and 188 living abroad. Replies were received from 191 Japanese and from 58 foreigners. Results of the poll are outlined below:

1. Almost all respondents (97.4% Japanese, 100% foreigners) gave a high appraisal of the plan for the information society. The reasons given by many of the Japanese and foreign respondents were the vision, purpose and the comprehensive nature of the plan.
2. On the question; 'Which of the nine projects listed in the intermediate impact program would have the strongest impact?', there were marked differences in ranking between the Japanese and foreign respondents.

Japanese respondents		Foreign respondents	
1. Broad-area medical care system	24%	Computopolis plan	30%
2. Administrative data bank	21%	Coumputer-oriented education system	17%
3. Broad-area anti-pollution system	19%	Broad-area anti-pollution system	14%
4. Computopolis plan	14%	Administrative data bank	12%
5. Computer-oriented education system	12%	Think-tank center	11%
Total	90%	Total	84%

The strong support of the 'computopolis plan' given by foreign respondents can be explained by its *high demonstration effect*. The high ranking for a 'computer-oriented experimental education system' given by foreign respondents is based on the recognition that education must *play an important role* in the development of the information society.

3. With respect to the emphasis placed by the kind on 'the intro- duction of information oriented systems into social areas', about 85 per cent of both the Japanese and foreign respondents sup- ported the concept. One said, 'I would pay tribute to Japan if Japan has succeeded in making the Vietnamese and the Chinese understand the significance of these social systems.'

4. Replies to the question 'Do you think that similar systems will be implemented in your country in the near future?' showed a time lag of about five years between the concepts of the Japanese and foreign respondents. As many as 70 per cent of the Japanese respondents expect that part of this plan would be *implemented* within five years, while 30 per cent of foreign respondents replied that such a plan would be *drawn up* within 10 years, and about 20 per cent of them said within 20 years. Countrywise, the percentage of those who took a negative attitude toward projects of this king was relatively higher in the United States, Britain and Italy, and was lower in Sweden and France. At the same time it is interesting to note that about 60 per cent of the respondents in the United States, the major home of free enterprise, recognized the pos- sibility of such planning in the future.

Many earnest comments and letters were sent by respondents to this international opinion poll.

> Human beings will face a crisis if we continue to extend the materialistic civilization. The Japanese information society plan is *one of the best solutions* to get through this serious crisis. *Robert Jungk* (Futurist, Austria)

> It is the result of *a considerable imaginative effort.* It tries to determine new, interesting, non-material objec- tives for mankind. The world should be grateful to the Japanese people for presenting so clearly issues which are vital to the future of mankind. *J.M. Gibb* (Assistant Director General, Commission of the European Com- munity, Luxemburg)

> The amount budgeted to global cooperation in the deve- lopment of the world information society reflects the im- portance of information as *a tool toward global interde- pendence.* For allocating resources to this humanistic

goal, Japan and the JCUDI deserve to be applauded.
J. Richardson (Acting Director, U.S. Department of
Commerce Office of Telecommunication, U.S.A.)

I think this plan is a magnificent effort at trying to
handle an entirely new emerging actual situation and a
social aspiration toward a new kind of society which is
basically concerned with *higher levels of self-actualization
of the individual. A.J. Dakin* (Professor of Urban and
Regional Planning, University of Toronto, Canada)

Results Accomplished under the Plan

The Japanese government's response to the plan for the information society system.

1. *In medicine;* preliminary research work was begun by the Ministry
   of Health and Welfare on a nationwide medical treatment information network (five-year plan, about ¥5,000 million) to connect all
   regional medical information centres throughout the country,
   and by the Ministry of International Trade and Industry on the
   development of medical treatment and examination systems
   (seven-year plan, about ¥30,000 million). These are long-term
   projects.
2. *In traffic control;* the Agency of Industrial Technology and
   Science has begun development of an automatic integrated traffic
   control system centering on mesh-type traffic information (five-
   year plan, ¥5,000 million), and the Economic Planning Agency
   CVS (computer-controlled vechicle system) and a system for un-
   manned operation of automobiles to be installed in the central
   parts of large cities (a 15-year plan, total budget about ¥90,000
   million).
3. Further, *in the area of transport;* the Ministry of Transport has
   worked out a long term plan (requiring an outlay, both governmental and private, of about ¥20,000 million by 1985) for the
   development of a three-dimensional (sea, air and land) transport
   information system with emphasis on safety in navigation and
   operation.
4. *In the area of urban development;* the Ministry of International
   Trade and Industry has already started model experiments on a
   CATV city, a two-way, multi-image, information system (seven-
   year plan, about ¥23,000 million). The Ministry has also decided
   to urge industrial enterprises broadly to present their plans for a

Table 1.1 Results Accomplished under the Information Society Plan

Names of projects	Degree of realization	Results accomplished
Administration data bank	◕	1. Operation of in-line data bank systems in almost all government agencies. 2. Mutual on-line utilization of data between Ministry of International Trade and Industry and Economic Planning Agency scheduled to start in 1979. 3. Start of time sharing commercial service of government data by NIEDS by Nihon Keizai Shimbun.
Computopolis plan	◑	1. Start of an experimental community communication information system in two new towns. 2. Completion of test on a CVS model, its practical application during OCEAN EXPO held in Okinawa, utilized by about 80,000 persons during the exposition period. 3. Development of an automated supermarket completed, and a model shop opened in Tokyo.
Broad area remote medical care systems	◕	1. Operation of emergency aid medical systems in 10 prefectures, including Osaka, Kanagawa. 2. Automated hospital system to start operation within 1979 between three national hospitals and Nippon Telegraph and Telephone Public Corp. 3. Networks of remote medical systems based on facsimile data transmission established in Niigata and Hokkaido, five experimental cases in doctorless villages in remote islands and areas. 4. In Nagano Prefecture, annually 50,000 persons are covered by regional health care systems, and Ministry of Health and Welfare has started a 10-year plan to increase the number of health care centers annually by 100.
Computer-oriented education in an experimental school	◑	1. A CAI (computer aided instruction) system model classroom is being tested at primary schools under the direction of Tsukuba University. 2. Training courses in computer operation and programming set up in public commercial high schools.
Pollution prevention system in a broad region	●	1. Establishment of a national pollution research institute and of 61 local pollution research institutes throughout the country. 2. Operation of pollution monitoring centers in Tokyo and other principal cities.
Think-tank center	◕	1. The National Institute for Research Advancement was established to make projections on energy and carry out large-scale research and studies on projects for the 21st century. 2. The Institute of Information Technology, Japan, was established to provide annually 60 courses for a total of about 1,000 persons.
MIS for small enterprises	●	1. The Central Information Center was set up, and 10 regional information centers were set up throughout the country.
Labor re-development center	○	None.
Computer peace corps	◕	1. Systems engineers and programmers dispatched to developing countries.

Notes:
●already realized, ◕in practical application, ◑in the stage of model tests, ○still to be undertaken.

demonstration project incorporating integrated social information systems such as a CVS and a CATV system, and community-wide heating and air-conditioning systems.

5. The National Institute for Research Advancement was established with joint investments by the Government and private enterprise as a *national center of think-tanks* to do integrated research and study. The fund for the purpose will ultimately be increased to a target amount of ¥30,000 million.

Unfortunately, these projects, all begun around the same time by government ministries, met with great difficulties because of the oil crisis around the end of the same year, and the Japanese economy, which had been experiencing a high growth rate, slowed to a low upward curve.

But in spite of these difficulties and unfavorable circumstances, not only the central Government, but also local governments, the Nippon Telegraph and Telephone Public Corporation, and private organizations, including the Machine Industry Promotion Association, separately undertook projects embodied in the Plan for the Information Society, each from its own independent standpoint, and promoted systems design, the development of equipment and model experiments.

It is now six years since the plan was proposed, and, with the exception of the project for establishing a labor redevelopment center, experiments in the other eight projects have been carried out or implemented in some form or other, and many even put to practical application. The result is that only two of the eight projects which were experimentally attempted or even put to practical use, viz., the computopolis plan and computer-oriented education in an experimental school, are still at the experimental stage, while four projects (administration data banks, broad area remote medical systems, think-tank centers and the computer peace corps) are already to the stage of practical application; the remaining two projects (pollution prevention system for a broad region, MIS of small enterprises) have reached the stage of expanded application. (See Table 1.1)

Among the various projects now under way, the Tama CCIS (Tama Coaxial Cable Information Systems)[5] and the *Hi-Ovis* (Higashi-Ikoma Optical Visual Information System)[6] have aroused world interest. These are two-way community information systems which combine computers with up-to-date communication technology, and can be considered as miniaturized prototypes of the information society of the future.

The Tama CCIS and the Hi-Ovis were initiated around the same time in 1971, under the guidance respectively of the Ministry of Posts and Telegraphs and the Ministry of International Trade and Industry, and in 1973 a Living Visual Information System Development Association was formed to unify the two projects. The Tama CCIS had already finished the stage of experimental operation by the end of 1978, while the Hi-Ovis experimental stage is scheduled to be completed by the end of 1980.

Tama CCIS

Tama New Town, centered about 30 kilometers from Tokyo, is planned for 90,000 households, comprising a population of 230,000 when completed. It was selected as an appropriate place where experiments (Tama CCIS) could be carried on for two years to provide the following 11 kinds of community information services for about 500 selected households. A total of $4 million was spent in laying the coaxial transmission lines.

Table 1.2 Contents of CCIS Services

11 services	Monitoring households
1. TV Retransmission Service	500
2. Original TV Telecasting Service	500
3. Automatic Repetition Telecasting Service	500
4. Pay TV Service	300
5. Flash Information Service	50
6. Facsimile Newspaper Service	20
7. Memo-Copy Service	30
8. Auxiliary Television Service	40
9. Broadcast and Response Service	80
10. Still Picture Request Service	80
11. Theft and Sisaster Prevention Service	100

Source: 'Tama CCIS Experiment Report', Living Visual Information System Development Association, Tokyo, 1978.

TV Retransmission Service: This service made it possible to offer ordinary TV broadcasts to the households with improved picture quality, and also enabled programs to be received which otherwise would have been unavailable.

Original TV Telecasting Service: A total of 1940 independent and original programs were telecast during the experimental period, providing (1) local news, (2) cultural and educational affairs, (3) information of living, (4) medical information, (5) entertainment, and others. Of these, 27 programs were produced by the people living in Tama new town. Participants in the programs from the monitoring households totaled 898 persons, accounting for about 30 per cent of all members of these households.

Automatic Repetition Telecasting Service: This is a 10-15 minute program consisting of 20-30 frames of characters, pictures and photographs, with recorded announcements. The telecasting of this program was repeated at certain intervals. As it is simple to prepare a program of this kind, a number of residents, especially *housewives, took an active part* in preparing them, with 260 programs prepared independently by the people. Seventeen housewives participated in this project as reporters throughout the experiment. Some titles used were, 'Set mirrors at curves and corners', 'We want doctors at night!' and 'Tests on reflection-type kerosene stoves'.

Pay TV Srevice: Two kinds of pay TV services were offered; the key type (operated by insertion of a special key) and the ticket type (operated by insertion of a special coupon).

Flash Information Service: Information in Japanese text was multiplexed with TV image information and displayed on TV screens like news flashes several times a day, with new content for each broadcast. These gave city news, sports news, weather forcasts and information directly related to living. During strikes on the private railways and after elections, information was given from time to time from early in the morning until late at night.

Facsimile Newspaper Service: Full sized pages of newspapers were automatically projected by home facsimile systems, for which purpose a transmitting station was set up inside the office of Asahi Shimbun (one of Japan's major dailies) in the central part of Tokyo. About 20 pages of the newspaper were transmitted from 7 in the morning until 5 in the evening. Special extras were transmitted to report on newsbreaking events, hijackings, and other incidents or accidents.

Memo-Copy Service: This was a one minute facsimile transmission of information received on recording paper, with a width of 10 cm. Transmissions were made to all the monitoring households simultaneously or to individuals or groups of households. Information provided concerned procedural matters and other guidance memos from the city office, the names of clinics and hospitals open on holidays, shopping guides for supermarkets, activities of circles, lectures, meetings, etc.

The reaction of the monitoring households to the memo-copy

service was very quick. When a certain store gave information on special bargain sales, using the memo-copy service, it was found that many people went at once to the store, with the result that the store had to extend the special sales periods. During the period of the experiment 87.5 per cent of the monitoring households made use of the tips given by this service on more than four days of the week.

Auxiliary Television Service: A pair of TV sets, one large and one small, were installed in the monitoring homes, with the smaller set used for giving emergency information (both video and audio) to the users. The emergency information concerned transport workers strikes, fires, typhoons, earthquakes, etc. This service was also used by the city office and the health care centers to call for blood donors when transfusions were needed and stocks were low. Emergency information was provided by this service on 76 occasions during the period of the experiment.

Broadcast and Response Service: This was a two-way inter-active service by which the subscriber with a keyboard-equipped audio terminal could ask questions and get replies from the broadcasting center dealing with programs transmitted by it, and even reply to questions from the center. In such cases, the center immediately tabulated the subscribers' replies and displayed them on the subscribers' TV screens. These programs included (1) educational matters, (2) various kinds of consultations, (3) questionnaires and (4) quizzes. In the educational programs the center offered English and Math lessons for the lower grades of primary school, and the children's mothers. In these programs, the teacher in the studio was able to converse with children and mothers in their homes, receive questions and give replies. Further, *public opinion polls* were taken by a Q and A system at the time of the dissolution of the Lower House and general election.

Still Picture Request Service: By this service the subscriber was able to have a desired still picture displayed on the TV screen on request, for which 6,300 pictures were prepared and kept in retrieval storage.

Results of the Experiment. Because of the restricted hours during which these services were offered, housewives were the largest number of utilize them, with children second. The number of husbands who utilized these services was half that of the housewives and children.

Evaluating the experiment as a whole, 62.9 per cent of the monitors said that the services were *meaningful* .

The evaluation of individual services placed the memo-copy service and the auxiliary TV service first, with both earnestly desired to be continued. By contrast, the still picture request service and the pay TV service, of which great expectations had been held before the start of the experiment, ranked lowest when the experiment ended. A possible reason is because the services were poor in content and because new information sources were not added.

In addition, in considering the kinds of information provided, programs on public services and the education were evaluated very highly. (See Table 1.3)

Both the central and local governments evaluated highly this CCIS, on the grounds that (1) it could be *an important infrastructure of a future community* and (2) that this system was an extremely effective means of enabling *the local residents to participate more fully in community activities.*

The cost of each service was estimated from the results of the experiment. This revealed that if there are 5,000 subscribers, the broadcasting type service (original TV broadcasting service, automatic repetition telecasting service) would cost ¥1,200 (about $6.00) a month, and the non-broadcasting service would be ¥4,000-¥8,000 ($20.00-$40.00) a month per household. If the number of households is increased to 20,000, the costs would come down to ¥322 ($1.60) for the former, and the non-broadcasting type to ¥3,000-¥6,000 ($15.00-$30.00). The subscribers expressed the desire that the charges for the services should be ¥500-¥1,000 ($2.50-¥5.00) per month per household, the difference in cost to be made up by central and/or local government subsidies, plus revenues from commercial advertising.

During the experimental period, more than 400 persons from about 40 other countries visited Tama New Town to observe the system at work. They were unanimous in praise of the system as an experiment of the world's most advanced community communication system, with many ideas for a future information society.

When the first stage experiment with the Tama CCIS was completed, it moved into the second experimental stage from early 1979, with the aim of full practical application.

In the second stage, (1) the kinds of services are limited to five, based on the results of the first stage: viz., automatic repetition telecasting, broadcasting and response, original TV broadcasting, flash information and memo-copy, (2) the number of subscribers will be increased to 3,000 by the end of 1980, with subscribers grouped according to school areas, and (3) charges for the services will begin in and after 1982 so that the entire system may be managed independently.

Table 1.3 Interest in, and Evaluation of, Tama CCIS Services

Ranking	Interest	Evaluation at the time of completion of experiment, September 1977			
	Before experiment March, 1975	Actual utility 'Useful'	Expectancy of usefulness 'Useful'	Desire for continued use (On condition of being gratis)	%
1	———	Memo-copy	Memo-copy	Memo-copy	85.0
2	———	Auxiliary TV	Auxiliary TV	Auxiliary TV	80.7
3	Still Picture Request	Flash Information	Facsimile Newspaper	Original TV Broadcasting	76.2
4	Flash Information	Facsimile Newspaper	Broadcasting and Response	Broadcasting and Response	75.8
5	Pay TV	Original TV Broadcasting	Flash Information	Flash Information	68.8
6	Automatic Repetition Telecasting	Broadcasting and Response	Original TV Broadcasting	Automatic Repetition Telecasting	61.8
7	Original TV Broadcasting	Automatic Repetition Telecasting	Automatic Repetition Telecasting	Facsimile Newspaper	50.0
8	Broadcasting and Response	Still Picture Request	Pay TV	Pay TV	48.3
9	Facsimile Newspaper	Pay TV	Still Picture Request	Still Picture Request	39.4

Note: Neither the memo-copy service nor the auxiliary TV service had been included in the original plan, so in the 'Before experiment' column, these items are blank.   Source: 'Tama CCIS Experiment Report,' March, 1978

Fig. 1.2 Tama CCIS: Prototype of the Living Visual Information System by Local Resident Participation

The Whole View of Tama New Town

Operating Room of Tama CCIS

Facsimile Newspaper Service

Pay TV Service

Original TV Telecasting Service

English Lesson Hour

The First Year Anniversary of Tama CCIS

Demonstration of Folk-Art Articles

Source: By Courtesy of the Living Visual Information System Development Association

Fig. 1.3 HI-Ovis: The World's First Experiment of Two-Way Multiplex Community Communications, Utilizing Optical Fiber Cable

HI-Ovis Head Quarters

Size of Optical Fiber Cable

Video Request Service

Still-Picture Service

TV Studio Broadcasting

A Composite Set at the User's End

"Let Us Discuss Education"

Demonstration of a Public Opinion Poll

Source: Same as Fig. 1.2

Hi-Ovis

The *Hi-Ovis* was completed in seven years from its inception, at Higashi-Ikoma New Town in Nara Prefecture, at a cost of $16 million, four times the amount spent on the Tama CCIS. This system is epoch-making, *the first major experiment* of its kind, a future living visual information city. It utilizes optical fiber cable instead of copper cable for two-way multiplex communication of video and audio signals and data. The community antenna is at the top of Mt. Ikoma, and the Hi-Ovis center links 158 households and 10 public institutions (schools, a fire station and the city office) with each other by means of optical fiber cable with a total length of 400 kilometers to form a communication network.

This system has the following three distinguishing features:

1. It is *the world's only optical fiber communication network put to practical use.* Optical fiber cable is capable of transmitting information several thousand times greater in quantity than the conventional copper cable of the same thickness, suffers little from interference and noise, and *prevents invasion of privacy* in communication. Theoretically speaking, users on this Hi-Ovis system can receive programs from 30 TV channels and calls from 1,000 telephone lines at the same time.
2. It permits *two-way multiplex communication by visual, audio and digital methods.* Unlike the Tama CCIS, (1) it does not use telephone lines, (2) not only the voice, but also the images of the users can be transmitted and received. For this purpose, a composite set that combines TV, a keyboard, a video camera and a microphone is installed at the user's end.
3. The Hi-Ovis city is *essentially a wired city.* No antenna rises from the roof, yet each user can receive TV images of good picture quality from the one community antenna.

The following four services are provided in the experiment:

a. TV retransmission service
b. Video request service
c. Still picture service
d. TV studio broadcasting

All these services were included in the Tama CCIS, but the services offered by Hi-Ovis are far richer in quantity and quality than those offered in the earlier experiment. For instance, a new channel is added to the TV retransmission service, and a new local program is prepared every week for the video request service, and it is planned to increase the number of video programs to 1,000 in the near future. Further, its still-picture service is more varied in content, including (1) local information (local emergency news, weather forecasts), (2) guide information (hospitals and clinics open on holidays, events, shows, etc.), (3) location information (schools, hospitals, etc.), (4) traffic information (traffic congestion, train schedules, etc.) and other similar items. The contents of these services are being constantly up-dated.

It is the last service, the TV studio broadcasting service, that is found to be the most important of all these services offered by the Hi-Ovis, in which the system gives full play to its excellent features.

For example, *the user can participate from home in a TV program by appearing on the screen, and speaking to other TV viewers and providing home data.* In other words, the user's own voice and image can be heard and seen on the TV screen as desired, and opinions can be recorded by digital signals in a public opinion poll. In this way the user can participate in a local discussion meeting, take part in foreign language lessons, ask and reply to questions, participate in quiz programs, charity auctions, etc., and thus participate in communication programs more actively than is possible under any other system.

For instance, in an educational program entitled 'Let Us Discuss Education' , on the NHK (Japan Broadcasting Association) TV network, Hi-Ovis was connected with the NHK network and two studios, one at NHK headquarters and the other at the Hi-Ovis center, were integrated, more than 500 kilometers apart. On the screen not only the panelists in the NHK studio but also those at the center spoke in turn. Then the participants in the program at the center replied to the moderator's questions by pressing their own push-buttons. Ninety per cent of the Hi-Ovis subscribers participated in this program.

It is still less than a year since these experimental services began, and it was found that monitor reactions were far more active than was the case with the Tama CCIS users. The main reason would be that a highly participatory program made by the studio and subscribers is offered every week by Hi-Ovis.

A plan is underway to present an optical communication system with 6,000 terminals at an international exhibition scheduled to be held in Kobe City in 1981. It is also planned to introduce an industrial information system based on optical transmission in Nishijin, Kyoto, where traditional Japanese Nishijin silk weaving is done.

2
Other Model Information Society Experiments

Examples of similar experimental projects are to be found in Canada and Sweden.

TELIDON Program (Canada)

The Department of Communication (DOC) and Bell Canada, reached agreement on August 28, 1979 for a co-operative $10 million venture that will help the development of one of the world's largest applications of the TELIDON[7] system (videotex is the internationally-recognized term). The first trial will see 1,000 user terminals, offering both residential and commercial users a choice of up to 100,000 'pages' of on-demand information for display on their own color television sets, come into operation by early 1981.

The Prestel service, offered by the British Post Office, is the world's first commercial two-way videodata service, and several countries, including the United States (RUBE system), Japan (CAPTAIN system) and France, are operating similar systems.

But these videotex systems are all first-generation 'alpha-mosaic'; only TELIDON is using the second-generation 'alpha-geometric' technology. TELIDON is more flexible and capable of easier accommodation, with superior quality resolution and graphics. The special technical capabilities of TELIDON are as follows:

- three dimensional solid images in color or in shades of grey to black
- can compose a specific image or message in random segments
- can put together the page following the one being read for 'multi-page'
- can adjust picture change speed to suit illustrated motion sequences

Since June 1979, some 150 prototype TELIDON systems have come into operation, and by September, the Ontario Educational Communications Authority, the Manitoba Telephone System, Alberta Government Telephones and two other institutions are committed to these trials.

DOC set up the application of social synergy for computer communications policy for TELIDON, and is helping to strengthen the available data base in provision of non-commercial fields of information. These include assisting federal departments to prepare relevant information, and more important, helping the community of educators to become expert in the use of TELIDON for both formal and recreational educational purposes.

The numerous public service and community applications include updated travel schedules, news, weather and sports headlines, stock market quotations, consumer bulletins, entertainment guides, classified ads and other yellow page type listings. Future potential applications will be emergency medical advice, career and employment information arranged for instant access by job categories, and covering the entire country, together with electronic directories, dictionaries, encyclopedias and other reference works.

The potential market is estimated at a total number of 200,000 subscribers to TELIDON by 1984 and 620,000 by 1986.

The greatest social significance of TELIDON is the possibility it offers for much wider access to information, and conversely, the much greater ease with which new concepts and ideas can be transmitted. The combination of computers and communications through TELIDON should lead to a further opening of the bureaucracies to the people's inspection and criticism, by disseminating information more quickly and more effectively. TELIDON should thus eliminate the need for many centralized decisions, and, if properly managed, provide a greater opportunity for more flexible rules and regulations.

Project TERESE (Sweden)

Another project with implications for computerization has been developed in Sweden. In 1975, the Swedish Expert Board for Regional Development and the National Board for Technical Development began a Project for Telecommunications and Regional Development, known as Project TERESE,[8] to analyse the possibilities of promoting desirable regional development by the use of telecommunications. This project is of special interest in relation to their theme of *voluntary action and synergy,* because the Working Group that has undertaken the study has concentrated the analysis on the needs of regions, as the group felt that technology should serve rather than control development. Contact was made with local governing bodies in order to identify the needs of regions, and then, in joint action with the central regional authorities, the group selected the Fyrkanten region in the North of Sweden, around the town of Lulea, for carrying out the experimental projects.

The logic behind the TERESE project is that the rapidly advancing telecommunications technology is more than simply a way of providing information rapidly and inexpensively; it has profound consequences for the whole of society. In the past, telecommunications technology has tended to reinforce the trend towards the centralized development of regions where investment had already been made. The TERESE project, however, aims at *a critical assessment of technology to determine* how telecommunications technology can be used to promote regional development, and in particular, to delineate and encourage technology that would otherwise be ignored because of short term market considerations.

A one-week preliminary seminar was held in Lulea in December, 1976, attended by local representatives of the areas of application. The seminar discussed:

- collective traffic
- distribution of consumer information
- planning by local authorities
- local citizen information
- efficient use of consultants
- factual business contacts between firms and markets
- computer aided and distributed education
- cooperative decision-making
- planning of local employment
- health systems communications
- communications for and between the handicapped

Participants had the opportunity to experience:

- computer conferencing
- computer aided education systems
- social question-answering computer application
  systems
    • health information and planning
    • psychiatric care
    • consumer information
    • planning of employment
- telephone conferencing

–tele-facsimile services
–picture telephone operation

During the seminar a number of project possibilities were developed, including some, interestingly enough, that were suggested initially by local representatives, not by the organizers. Later, a number of projects were selected for further study, including:

- *Promotion of local small businesses.* This project deals with increased interaction within small firm conglomerates, aimed at giving small business firms at peripheral locations some of the advantages of resource sharing normally confined to larger and more densely populated urban centers.
- *Joint planning for northern Nordic regions.* This project would link up the northern regions of Sweden, Norway, and Finland to promote joint utilization of resources.
- *Health care.* This stresses information distribution in rural environments, including local planning of mobile nurses, and resource pooling of specialist knowledge between different regional hospitals.
- *Distributed education.* This provides for the use of simple telecommunication aids for dissemination of education.
- *Increased communication for the handicapped.* Computer supported typewriter terminals, for example, to provide new communication patterns for people with impaired hearing.
- *Telecommunications and reduction of energy consumption.* Reducing energy consumption through the use of telecommunications as a substitute for travel.

A local organization was formed for the evaluation of practical applications according to these project specifications.

The projects were evaluated in 1978—79, taking into consideration social and psychological as well as the technical aspects. Two main conclusions were reached:

- *The social introduction of terminal oriented systems needs special observation,* especially in cases of previously non-educated citizens being exposed to new service possibilities.
- *There are boundaries to the size of the project* that

have to be overcome before a meaningful evaluation
will be possible for such projects.

For 1980, the projects are being concentrated into two main areas:

–Distance education
–Information for small scale industries

The expanded evaluation of these projects will take place in 1981.
The TERESE project is particularly interesting in its practical approach, in the emphasis it places on *social welfare,* and in the cooperation it promotes, particularly in *the joint planning with other
countries* to promote the future development of the northern regions.

3
Image of the Future Information Society

What is the image of the information society? The composition of the concept will be built on the following two premises:

1. The information society will be a new type of human society, completely different from the present industrial society. Unlike the vague term 'post-industrial society', the term 'information society' as used here will describe in concrete terms the characteristics and the structure of this future society. The basis for this assertion is that *the production of information values and not material values will be the driving force* behind the formation and development of society. Past systems of innovational technology have always been concerned with material productive power, but the future information society must be built within a completely new framework, with a thorough analysis of the system of computer-communications technology that determines the fundamental nature of the information society.
2. The developmental pattern of industrial society is the societal model from which we can predict the overall composition of the information society. Here is another bold 'historical hypothesis': *the past developmental pattern of human society can be used as a historical analogical model for future society.*
   Putting the components of the information society together piece by piece by using this historical analogy is an extremely effective way for building the fundamental framework of the information society.

The Overall Composition of the Information Society

Table 3.1 presents the overall framework of the information society based upon these two premises. This table presents the overall composition of the information society based on a historical

Table 3.1 Pattern Comparison of Industrial Society and the Information Society

		INDUSTRIAL SOCIETY	INFORMATION SOCIETY
Innovational Technology	Core	Steam engine (power)	Computer (memory, computation, control)
	Basic function	Replacement, amplification of physical labor	Replacement, amplification of mental labor
	Productive Power	Material productive power (increase in per capita production)	Information productive power (increase in optimal action-selection capabilities)
Socio-economic structure	Products	Useful goods and services	Information, technology, knowledge
	Production center	Modern factory (machinery, equipment)	Information utility (information networks, data banks)
	Market	New world, colonies, consumer purchasing power	Increase in knowledge frontiers, information space
	Leading industries	Manufacturing industries (machinery industry, chemical industry)	Intellectual industries, (information industry, knowledge industry)
	Industrial structure	Primary, secondary, tertiary industries	Matrix industrial structure (primary, secondary, tertiary, quaternary/systems industries)
	Economic Structure	Commodity economy (division of labor, separation of production and consumption)	Synergetic economy (joint production and shared utilization)
	Socio-economic principle	Law of price (equilibrium of supply and demand)	Law of goals (principle of synergetic feedforward)
	Socio-economic subject	Enterprise (private enterprise, public enterprise, third sector)	Voluntary communities (local and informational communities)
	Socio-economic system	Private ownership of capital, free competition, profit maximization	Infrastructure, principle of synergy, precedence of social benefit
	Form of society	Class society (centralized power, classes, control)	Functional society (multicenter, function, autonomy)
	National goal	GNW (gross national welfare)	GNS (gross national satisfaction)
	Form of government	Parliamentary democracy	Participatory democracy
	Force of social change	Labor movements, strikes	Citizens' movements, litigation
	Social problems	Unemployment, war, fascism	Future shock, terror, invasion of privacy
	Most advanced stage	High mass consumption	High mass knowledge creation
Values	Value standards	Material values (satisfaction of physiological needs)	Time-value (satisfaction of goal achievement needs)
	Ethical standards	Fundamental human rights, humanity	Self-discipline, social contribution
	Spirit of the times	Renaissance (human liberation)	Globalism (symbiosis of man and nature)

analogy from industrial society. Let me explain each of the major items. Of course the entire picture of the future information society can not be given at this stage, but at least this table will help the reader understand the composition and overall relations between chapters that unfold later in the book[9].

1. The prime innovative technology at the core of development in industrial society was the steam engine, and its major function was to substitute for and amplify the physical labor of man. In the information society, 'computer technology' will be the innovational technology that will constitute the developmental core, and its fundamental function will be to *substitute for and amplify the mental labor of man.*

2. In industrial society, the motive power revolution resulting from the invention of the steam engine rapidly increased material productive power, and made possible the mass production of goods and services and the rapid transportation of goods. In the information society, 'an information revolution' resulting from development of the computer will rapidly expand information productive power, and make possible *the mass production of cognitive, systematized information, technology, and knowledge.*

3. In industrial society, the modern factory, consisting of machines and equipment, became the societal symbol and was the production center for goods. In the information society *the information utility* (a computer-based public infrastructure) consisting of information networks and data banks will replace the factory as *the societal symbol,* and become the production and distribution center for information goods.

4. Markets in industrial society expanded as a result of the discovery of new continents and the acquisition of colonies. The increase in consumption purchasing power was the main factor in expansion of the market. In the information society, 'the knowledge frontier' *will become the potential market,* and the increase in the possibilities of problem solving and the development of opportunities in a society that is constantly and dynamically developing will be the primary factor behind the expansion of the information market.

5. In industrial society, the leading industries in economic development are machinery and chemicals, and the total structure comprises primary, secondary, and tertiary industries. In the information society the leading industries will be *the intellectual industries,* the core of which will be the knowledge industries. *Information-related industries* will be newly added as *the quaternary group* to the industrial structure of primary, secondary, and

tertiary. This structure will consist of a matrix of information-related industries on the vertical axis, and health, housing and similar industries on the horizontal axis.

6. The economic structure of industrial society is characterized by (1) a sales-oriented commodity economy, (2) specialization of production utilizing divisions of labor, (3) complete division of production and consumption between enterprise and household. In the information society (1) information, the axis of socio-economic development, will be produced by the information utility, (2) self-production of information by users will increase; information will accumulate, (3) this accumulated information will expand through synergetic production and shared utilization and (4) the economy will change structurally from an exchange economy to *a synergetic economy.*

7. In industrial society the law of price, the universal socio-economic principle, is the invisible hand that maintains the equilibrium of supply and demand, and the economy and society as a whole develop within this economic order. In the information society *the goal principle* (a goal and means principle) will be the fundamental principle of society, and the synergetic feedforward, which apportions functions in order to achieve a common goal, will work to maintain the order of society.

8. In industrial society, the most important subject of social activity is the enterprise, the economic group. There are three areas: private enterprise, public enterprise, and a third sector of government ownership and private management. In the information society the most important subject of social activity will be *the voluntary community,* a socio-economic group that can be broadly divided into local communities and informational communities.

9. In industrial society the socio-economic system is a system of private enterprise characterized by private ownership of capital, free competition, and the maximization of profits. In the information society, the socio-economic system will be a voluntary civil society characterized by the superiority of its infrastructure, as a type of both public capital and knowledge-oriented human capital, and by a fundamental framework that embodies *the principle of synergy and social benefit.*

10. Industrial society is a society of centralized power and hierarchical classes. The information society, however, will be a multi-centered and complementary voluntary society. It will be horizontally functional, maintaining social order by *autonomous and complementary functions of a voluntary civil society.*

11. The goal of industrial society is to establish a Gross National Welfare Society, aiming to become a cradle-to-grave high welfare

society. The information society will aim for *the realization of time value* (value that designs and actualizes future time), for each human being. The goal of society will be for everyone to enjoy a worthwhile life in the pursuit of greater future possibilities.

12. The political system of industrial society is a parliamentary system and majority rule. In the information society the political system will become a *participatory democracy.* It will be the politics of participation by citizens; the politics of autonomous management by citizens, based on agreement, participation and synergy that take in the opinions of minorities.

13. In industrial society, labor unions exist as a force for social change, and labor movements expand by the use of labor disputes as their weapon. In the information society, *citizen movements* will be the force behind social change; their weapons will be litigation and participatory movements.

14. In industrial society there are three main types of social problems: recession-induced unemployment, wars resulting from international conflict, and the dictatorships of fascism. The problems of the information society will be future shocks caused by the inability of people to respond smoothly to rapid societal transformation, acts of individual and group terrorists such as hijackings, *invasions of individual privacy* and the crisis of *a controlled society.*

15. The most advanced stage of industrial society is a high mass consumption stage, centering on durable goods, as evidenced by motorization (the diffusion of the automobile). The most advanced stage of the information society will be *the high mass knowledge creation society,* in which computerization will make it possible for each person to create knowledge and to go on to self-fulfillment.

16. In industrial society, the materialistic values of satisfying physiological and physical needs are the universal standards of social values; but in the information society, seeking *the satisfaction of achieved goals* will become the universal standard of values.

17. Finally, the spirit of industrial society has been the renaissance spirit of human liberation, which ethically means respect for fundamental human rights and emphasis on the dignity of the individual, and a spirit of brotherly love to rectify inequalities.
    The spirit of the information society will be *the spirit of globalism, a symbiosis in which man and nature* can live together in harmony, consisting ethically of *strict self-discipline and social contribution.*

Fig. 3.1   Transformation Process from Industrial Society to Information Society

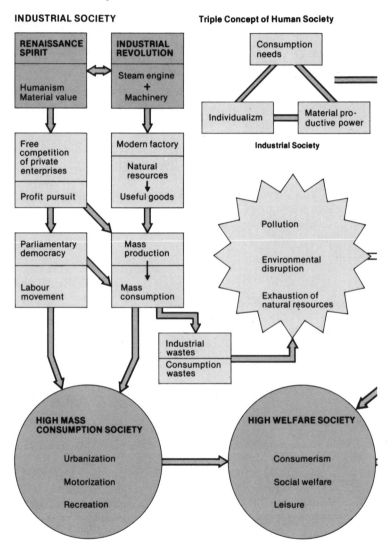

INFORMATION SOCIETY

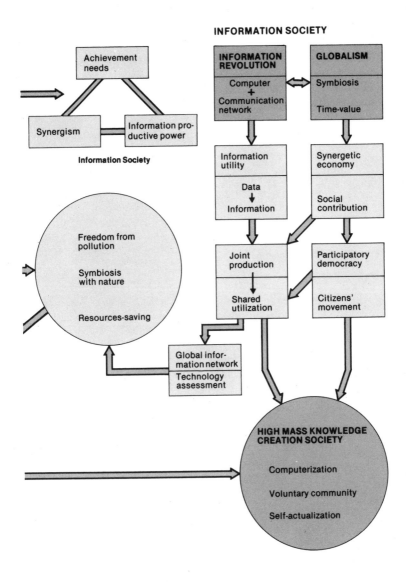

Information Society

4
When Will the Information Society Be Realized?

In considering the question of when the information society will become a reality, we first have to look at the stages of development in computerization, utilization and popularization of computers in society, and try to decide what the current stage of development is, and from this to predict when computerization will reach its final stage.

The Four Developmental Stages of Computerization

Table 4.1 breaks down the development of computerization according to the areas affected. There are four stages based respectively on the use of computers at the level of (1) big science, (2) management, (3) society, and (4) the individual.[10]

First Stage—Big Science-Based Computerization
The first stage in the development of *computerization* took place in the period between around 1945 and 1970, which we will call the stage of big science. This refers to the period in which the computer began to be used extensively in national scale projects, such as national defense and space exploration. In this case, the state (a subject) carried out computerization. Placing national prestige at stake, countries undertook the development of large scale systems for national defense and for landing men on the moon. The United States took the lead, and used the computer extensively for SAGE (Semi-Automatic Ground Environment System), protection against missile attack from the Soviet Union, in national defense, and for the Apollo program in space exploration.

In the Apollo space program the computer was put to use extensively in systems technology, in calculating trajectories and in remote control of space-craft between the earth and the moon.

Table 4.1   The Developmental Stages of Computerization

Stage of Development	First Stage 1945-1970	Second Stage 1955-1980	Third Stage 1970-1990	Fourth Stage 1975-2000
Bases of Computer Usage	Big Science	Management	Society	Individual
Goal	National defense, space exploration	Gross national product (GNP)	Gross national welfare (GNW)	Gross national satisfaction (GNS)
Values	National prestige	Economic growth	Social welfare	Self-actualization
Subject	Nation	Organizations	General public	Individual
Object of computer use	Nature	Organization	Society	Human beings
Scientific base	Natural sciences	Management sciences	Social sciences	Behavioral sciences
Information object	Attaining scientific goals	Pursuing business efficiency	Solving social problems	Intellectual creation

Source: Japan Computer Usage Development Institute 'The plan for information society'

Second Stage—Management-Based Computerization

The base of computerization in *the second stage* has moved from big science-based to *management-based computerization* in both government and business. This stage that extends from around 1955 to about 1980.

Unlike stage (1), in the second stage the expansion of GNP will be important. As computerization is applied to the areas of management and administration in both government and private enterprise, the use of the computer will be to improve the efficiency of operations of such bodies.

The development and use of management information systems (MIS), in which management and information sciences are linked, will advance.

In this second stage also, the United States has led the way, because the large-scale national defense and space information systems developed in the first stage have now been introduced into management and administration in big business and government. Big business in particular has made extensive use of the technology and systems developed by the government for national defense and space exploration. The SAGE system, for example, developed into the SABER system for passenger reservations in air travel, and the global inventory control system, developed for world military bases of the United States, has also been used by multinational corporations for inventory management on an international scale. Further, the methods of operations research developed during World War II have been used in management optimization.

With the development of methods also, such as systems analysis and PPBS, the computer has come to be used by national and state governments as a powerful weapon in the making of complex policy.

Third Stage—Society-Based Computerization

Computerization is now advancing to *the third stage, society-based computerization,* in which the computer will be used for the benefit of society as a whole. Society-based computerization has been advancing since 1970, and will probably go on through 1990, with many uses of the computer being applied to a *wide range of social needs.*

As this happens, GNW (gross national welfare) will become the goal instead of increases in the GNP (gross national product). The use of the computer will be for resolving problems in all areas of society, involving citizens as a whole. Thus *the general public will have a major role in the application of computerization at the level of the ordinary people.*

Of course national and local governments will be responsible to determine policy in computer applications, but decisions regarding subjects will actually be made by the people, who will be directly affected by computerization at society level. At this stage, the social and interdisciplinary sciences, in combination with information networks, will be used extensively to solve complex social problems.

Take medicine, for example. New medical systems, such as medical care systems for remote places, and regional health management systems, can be brought under the computer system.

The educational system will be different from the present standard school education. *A knowledge network* will become the core of a new type of education, which places the emphasis on individual abilities. New social information systems will make use of the computer networks in a variety of social fields, covering matters such as pollution, traffic, and problems of distribution. This third stage, therefore, has become the stage of computerization for the service of society at large, and in many countries this stage was entered during the 1970's.

Fourth Stage—Individual-Based Computerization

Computerization is now entering its *fourth stage of individual-based computerization*, made possible by the invention of integrated circuits. It will probably enter this stage fully between the years 1975 to 2000. Computerization thus advances from the level of society at large to the individual level. Each person will be able to use computer information obtained from *man-machine* systems (systems in which dialogue between man and the computer is carried on by a conversational mode), to resolve problems and to pursue the new possibilities of the future.

At this stage, the information society will have reached the equivalent level of the most advanced stage of industrial society, the high mass consumption stage in which the people have durable goods of the television and automobile types. The ready availability of information and knowledge will cause creativity to flourish among the people, the highest level of computerization, which I call *the high mass knowledge creation society*. At this stage there will be a personal terminal in each household, used to solve day-to-day problems and determine the direction of one's future life. Such computerization will not be carried out by large organizations, but by each individual. *Each person will be the subject who carries out computerization*, and as this is done, great advances will be seen in the behavioral sciences.

I must add, in conclusion, that these four stages can not be a series of mere successive developments, but each stage will continue developing even while the succeeding stage is coming into being.

Computerization from the Standpoint of Information Space

Having looked at the development of computerization according to each level of application, let us look at computerization from the viewpoint of information space and see how far it has already come. By information space we present the concept of the use of computer information spatially, referring to the range of a computer information network.

The expansion of this information space will go through three stages. The first will be the stage of limited space; the second, the stage of regional-national space, the third, the stage of global space. The current stage of development in computerization can be comprehended by combining these three stages of development with the previous four stages of development in the areas of application. Table 4.2. sets out the developmental process for computerization in these terms.

Table 4.2   Stages of Computerization from the Standpoint of Information Space

	Big Science	Management	Society	Individual
Limited space (computer)	Trajectory calculations	Management information systems	Library information retrieval system	Electronic calculators
		Numerical control systems	CAI education systems	Home computers
Regional-national space (computer + communications circuits)	SAGE system (Semi-automatic ground environment system)	Ticket reservation systems	Coordinated traffic control systems	Push button telephone service
		On-line banking systems	Regional pollution prevention systems	CATV systems
		Commercial T.S.S. (Time Sharing system)	Regional medical care systems	Videodata systems Information utilities
Global space (computer + communications circuits + Communications satellites)	Apollo Space Program ERTS (Earth Resources Technology Satellite)	Multinational management information systems	PEACESAT (Pacific Education and communications System)	Global information utilities
		World food information systems	Global Medical care systems	

First Stage—Computerization in Limited Space

The first stage, computerization in *limited space,* refers to restricted use of the computer by a business enterprise, a government, or a household, with the core technology advanced no further than the computer. Examples of this are in big science, the calculation of missile trajectories by the military, and the numerical calculations of atomic physics in universities and research centers. At management level, there are many examples of statistical tasks involved in compilation of a national census by the government, production control in factories, and the mass of routine calculations necessary to organizations. At society level, there are information retrieval services in libraries and CAI education in schools. And at an individual level, we can point to the existence of electronic calculators (the IC chip is a key component of the computer), home computers, and TV games.

Second Stage—Computerization in Regional-National Space
The second stage of spatial development in computerization is in *regional-national space*. This refers to the range of information networks by which enterprises, government organizations, local governments, and individuals carry on mutual exchanges and the shared use of computer information. For this stage, the computer must be combined with communications circuits.

Examples include, at the level of big science, the early introduction by the military of national defense systems such as SAGE. The use of the computer by the military shows how suitable the computer has always been for use in networks. At the managerial level, there are the examples of the SAGE system being taken over by private enterprise in the passenger reservation systems of airlines and the on-line banking systems. The TSS (Time sharing services) for business can also be included in this stage. And in Japan, in September 1970, the society finally reached this level with the opening of the communications circuits to businesses. Examples at the society level are the coordinated traffic control systems, pollution monitoring, prevention and elimination systems, and regional emergency medical care systems. The formation of regional-national information space at the level of society is just coming into being in many countries.

Finally, at the individual level, there are the examples of the pushphone, CATV, and the *wired city*. Experimental projects of community communication visual information systems began in Japan in the Tama New Town and Higashi Ikoma projects of 1976.

There are also *videodata systems* by which subscribers are able to dial up a computer by telephone and have information displayed on their own TV screens. This is at the experimental stage in England since 1978, and many other countries, including the U.S.A., Canada and Japan, have begun the same project in concert.

These movements suggest that the era of information utility is really at hand.

Third Stage—Computerization in Global Space
The third stage refers to *computerization in Global space*. Communication satellites are added to the information technology of computer and communications circuits. At the level of big science, this stage has already been entered. The series of back-up systems for the Apollo Program and ERTS (Earth Resources Technology Satellite) are typical examples. ERTS is proving to be particularly effective in the search for underground resources. At the managerial level, a global information service using communication satellites has already been put into operation by General Electric, and many

American multinational corporations have begun to operate their own global management information systems. At the level of society, computerization has not yet escaped from the experimental stage, and has scarcely moved beyond PEACESAT (Pacific Education and Communications Experiment by Satellite) an experiment in implementing an educational information system in the Pacific Basin.

On an individual level, computerization appears to still be no more than a phantasmal picture of the future. But as we enter the 21st century, which is not far away, *global information utilities* will become realities, and people in any part of the world will be able to utilize these GIUs as freely as we now use international telephones.

It will be possible for people all over the world to obtain services ranging from self-education systems, library information systems, to enjoy competitive games, and to *participate in a global voting* system to deal with such issues as atomic power generation.

A Comparison of the Tempo of the Motive Power Revolution and the Information Revolution

Let us seek a clearer idea of when the information society will come into being by using various indices to make a comparison between the tempo of the motive power revolution of industrial society and the information revolution of the information society. The comparison has shown that the latter revolution has occurred three to six times faster than the motive power revolution, it can be predicted that the high mass knowledge creation society, the most advanced stage of the information age, will probably be actualized somewhere on earth by the middle of the twenty-first century (See Table 4.3).

Let us look at the dates of technological innovations that have played decisive roles in the power revolution. Thomas Newcomen invented the first steam engine in 1708, and James Watt improved the Newcomen engine and completed the first operable steam engine in 1775. The first railroad was laid between Liverpool and Manchester in 1829, and the production of the Model-T Ford, the first car on the mass market, began in 1909. The jet plane emerged in 1937. There was a period of 229 years in technological development between the invention of the Newcomen engine and the emergence of the jet plane.

Note the contrast in the computer revolution. ENIAC, the first vacuum tube computer (first generation computer), was developed by two scientists, Eckert and Mauchly in 1946. The second generation computer, using transistors, was developed in 1956; the third generation computer, which utilized integrated circuits, appeared in 1965.

Table 4.3   A Comparison of the Tempo of the Motive Power Revolution and the Information Revolution

	A. Motive Power Revolution		B. Information Revolution		Ratio A/B
Advancement of technology	Newcomen engine	1708 ⎫	First generation computer	1946 ⎫	
	Steam engine	1775 ⎬ 229 years	Second generation computer	1956 ⎬ 36 years	
	Railroad	1829 ⎭	Third generation computer	1965 ⎭	6.4:1
	Automobile	1909	Micro-processor	1973	
	Jet plane	1937	Fourth generation computer	1982	
Diffusion of core machinery and systems	1,500 Steam engines 1708 / 1800	92 years	30,000 Computers 1946 / 1966	20 years	4.6:1
	1,000 Power looms 1784 / 1833	49 years	Automatic data processing 1946 / 1955	9 years	5.4:1
Industrial development	Construction of American transcontinental railroad 1828 / 1869	41 years	Formation of an American nationwide information network 1965 / 1972	7 years	6.0:1
	Establishment of manufacturing industries 1708 / 1909	201 years	Establishment of information industries 1946 / 1990	44 years	4.6:1
Societal development	High mass consumption society 1708 / 1930	222 years	High mass knowledge creation society 1946 / (?)2010	64 years	3.5:1

Microprocessors, integrated circuits on one chip, appeared in 1973, and now the development of the VLSI (very large scale integrated circuits) is underway. Success seems assured, and that the fourth generation of computers will come into practical use early in the 1980's.

Technological developments in the motive power revolution from the Newcomen to the jet engine took approximately 230 years, but in the information revolution, the period from the first generation to the fourth generation computer, will probably not be more than some 36 years. The information revolution will have occurred about 6.4 times faster than the power revolution.

Looking at the diffusion of the core machinery and systems in each case, we find that the motive power revolution took 57 years for the development of the Newcomen engine to reach 1000 units, and a further 35 years for James Watt's engine to spread throughout modern industry, such as steel, coal mining, and spinning. Together, this adds up to 82 years. In 20 years from the development of the computer, more than 30,000 machines were put into operation throughout the world. The diffusion of the computer has taken place about 4.6 times faster than the diffusion of steam engine power.

Take another example. It took 49 years for the first 1000 power-equipped spinning machines to be sold, but it took only 9 years for data processing by computers to be introduced into business. Automatic data processing has moved 5.4 times faster than the diffusion of power-equipped spinning machines.

When we look at industrial development, we see that it took 41 years for railroads to achieve the construction of the American transcontinental railroad, but only 7 years were needed for an information network to cover the same American continent, six times faster than the railroads. If manufacturing industries became 'leading industries' with the establishment of the automobile industry, then the development from the Newcomen engine took 201 years. The 'leading industry' to be developed from the computer will be the information industry. While the information industry is still in the process of formation, we can expect that its position as an industry will be established by about 1990, which means a development over 44 years, which is 4.6 times faster than the development of the manufacturing industries.

Finally, let us look at societal development. We have referred to the most advanced stage of industrial society, brought into being by the motive power revolution, as the high mass consumption society. If this is regarded as coinciding with the spread of motorization in a high mass consumption society, then this stage was reached in America in 1930, 222 years after the introduction of the Newcomen engine. It will take quite some time for the high mass knowledge creation society to emerge as the most advanced stage of the information society. If this is regarded as coinciding with the joint utilization of information utilities by the people, this stage will be reached by the end of the first decade of the 21st century, about 3.5 times as fast as the development of industrial society.

It should be clear now that whichever of these four indices one uses, the speed of the information revolution will be between three and six times the rate of development of the motive power revolution.

PART TWO
FRAMEWORK OF THE INFORMATION SOCIETY

Life is so rich
making dreams come true
beyond the satisfaction
of today's needs
to grasp time-values
and create the design
etched
upon the future's
invisible canvas

—Andrew Hughes—

5
The Information Epoch: Quiet Societal Transformation

A. Why Computer-Communications Technology Will Bring about an Information Epoch

Mankind is in the process of a quiet societal transformation; the opening of an information epoch centering on computer technology operating in conjunction with communications technology. An 'information epoch'[11] is *the span of time during which there is an innovation in information technology that becomes the latent power of societal transformation that can bring about an expansion in the quantity and quality of information and a large-scale increase in the stock of information.*

This information epoch centering on computer technology will have a far more decisive impact on human society than the 'power' revolution that began with the invention of the steam engine. The basic reason is that the fundamental function of the computer is to substitute for and amplify human mental work, whereas the steam engine had the basic function of substituting and amplifying physical labor.

The world's first computer, ENIAC, was invented by J. P. Eckert and J. W. Mauchly, in 1946, 171 years after James Watt's steam engine of 1775. The invention of ENIAC was motivated by military needs, the need for high-speed calculation of flight characteristics of projectiles for military purposes. This machine was essentially different from the tools or machines that had so far been invented, in that it had a mechanical calculating brain.

The importance of computer technology is in the fact that *for the first time a machine was made to create and supply information.* The computer was an epochal machine of logic, equipped with the three information processing functions of memory, computation and control, which greatly increased human ability to originate information.

The Complete Objectification of Information

The computer has three tremendously superior characteristics as a man-made intelligence machine.

The first is *the complete objectification of information.* The complete objectification of information means (1) production of information independent of human beings, (2) the originality of information thus produced, and (3) its storage in preservable forms. It can be said that this objectification of information is an index to progress in the structure of information. Mankind carried out the first information revolution as a revolution in language, but at this stage, information could not be objectified, which means *the separation of information from its subject.* Information was simply transmitted from A to B and had not become independent of man. Objectification of information began with the advance of production technology that brought it to the stage of written information. In the forms of alphabet and ideograms man first inscribed information on stone, which was thus transmitted to a third party in a completely independent, objectified form. This can be called *primary objectification.*

When the information revolution reached the stage of the printing revolution, objectified written information was disseminated in multiform reproduction by the printing press, and became typographically recorded information. This meant that information was objectified at a second level, with the shift from written to typographical information, *the secondary objectification.* As the information revolution progressed, the tendency towards separation and objectification of information increased further. The computer revolution has not simply advanced this objectification of information another step; it has carried out a critical qualitative leap by completely separating the production of information from the subjects, so that the production of information moves from man to machine. I call this objectification *the tertiary objectification* of information. Figure 5. 1 sets out this process. As the figure shows, primary objectification occurred at the stage of written information, the secondary objectification took place at the stage of printed information, and the tertiary objectification was initiated with the electronic processing of information. At this stage the production of information by a machine begins, and the complete objectification of information is achieved.

The process of objectification of information may be likened to mankind's progress in knowledge. The invention of written characters as the first form of objectification of information made it possible for the first time in human history to preserve information in

Fig. 5.1 Objectification Process of Information

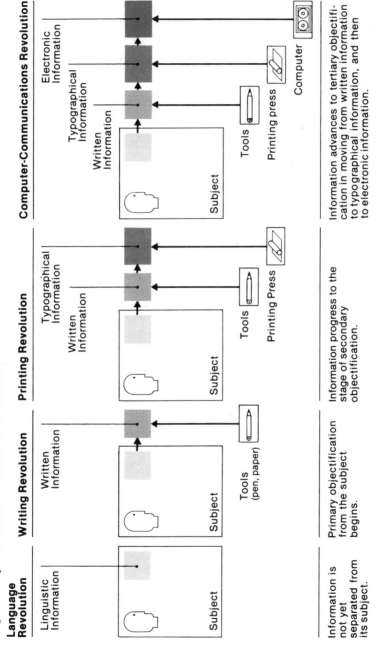

the form of objective existence. This led to the systematic development of technology and the formation of a composite body of knowledge, and the creation of poetry and literature. Further, the development of printing as the second-stage objectification of information led to the copying of information by machines, making it possible to greatly speed up the production of information, bringing in its wake the mass production and mass distribution of information and knowledge, the popularization of literature and knowledge, and the widespread dissemination of information by the press and other mass media.

Furthermore, the invention of the computer as the third objectification of information has made it possible to produce original information by a machine. The computer also has the functions of memory, calculation and control, operating as a mechanical brain. The development of the computer can thus replace the production of information by man, by means of automation of the production of information and substantially amplifying man's intellectual capacity through man-machine type utilization of computers.

Production of Sophisticated Cognitive Information

The second great characteristic is *the production of sophisticated cognitive information.*

The computer does not merely produce information; it produces sophisticated *cognitive information.* Here 'cognitive information' refers to information that is *a projection of the future;* it is *logical,* and it is *action-selective.* The projection means that the cognitive information is used for detecting and forecasting. 'Logical' signifies *the existence of a goal and ends relationship; cause and effect within cognitive information,* and 'action-selective' means that the information is used for *the selection of actions and means most appropriate for achieving a goal.* The fact that the computer can produce this cognitive information mechanically and in large quantities is a great contribution to the amplification of mental labor.

The primates, including man, make full use of two kinds of information to sustain and enrich the content of their living. One is cognitive information and the other *affective information.* 'Affective information' refers to information that is based on *sensitivity and production of emotion.* It embraces all the information that conveys sensory feelings, such as 'comfort,' 'pain' and the emotional feelings of 'happy' and 'sad'. These two kinds of information operate like two wheels of a car, and both are essential for human living. But it is the knowlege-oriented information that plays the decisive role in the progress and development of human society. 'Emotional information', to put it precisely, is from the beginning an expression of emotional life that is *simply for an organism's own use satisfaction,* not the sort of information that brings about an active change in the situational relationship between a subject and the object around it.

'Cognitive information', on the other hand, *makes possible purposeful action-selection in response to changes in situational relations.* Cognitive information, in other words, makes possible the active interaction with the external environment, resulting in change, from which progress takes place in the life of mankind.

The Information Cycle. In protozoans there is a prototype of cognitive information, which seems to indicate that cognitive intofmation came into being with the very origin of life. The fundamental characteristic of an organism is that it takes in food to sustain its existence, and carries on reproduction in order to continue the species. Thus an organism seems predestined to be forever acting on the external environment, looking for food, and protecting itself from external enemies. Here cognitive information plays an indispensable role.

A *situational relation* exists between the organism and the environment surrounding it. The 'situational relation' is *the relation between a subject and an object that comes into being in a particular situation,* and to which there are three conditions: (1) there must be a subject and an object (in this case the environment surrounding the subject), (2) the subject must receive impulses from the object, and (3) the subject takes action in response to these impulses. More noteworthy, however, is the pattern of action that is visible

Fig.5.2 The Information Cycle

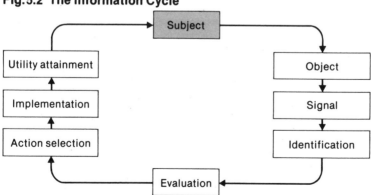

in the living protozoan. A protozoan uses organelles to ingest food and reject alien matter in response to signals received from outside. The four continuous steps that can be seen in the simplest actions of protozoans, *subject—object—signal—action,* constitute the fundamental structure of cognitive information, which we can call 'the information cycle'.

The *information cycle* is shown in Figure 5. 2. The subject receives a signal from the object, identifies the signal and evaluates it according to an acquired standard of judgement, selects a course of action, and finally achieves some use value by implementing the action.

The Function of Information. In order to understand the information cycle more clearly, we can take the example of the amoeba, and examine it in detail. In this information cycle the subject (the amoeba) first receives signals from the object (external environment) by means of its organelles. There are four types of signals provided by nature; physical and chemical, temperature, light, acid and alkali. The amoeba does not simply receive these signals; it distinguishes between them qualitatively and quantiatively.

The amoeba responds to change in the frequency of these signals when it selects a course of movement and transfers this into action. It moves, for example, in response to a change in temperature indicating warmth or cold. It distinguishes between differences of temperature as subtle as one twentieth of a degree per cubic centimeter of water surrounding it, and accordingly changes the direction of its movement. Obviously the amoeba has some sort of standard by which it evaluates the quantitative changes of these signals. This becomes even more apparent when one looks at the amoeba's intake of liquid food; it takes in liquids as well as solids. The liquid it selects to ingest is according to the type of liquid. It also takes in salts and proteins and expels carbohydrates and nucleic acids. The concentration of salts which can most readily be absorbed is one tenth of a mole.[12]

The Utility of Cognitive Information. Let us look at the process by which cognitive information is utilized. We have seen that (1) the amoeba selects some actions (action selection) to take in food when a signal indicates that food is there, and that (2) successful implementation of this action secures life support for the amoeba. The value of the signal the amoeba receives is that it is useful in selecting an action that will maintain the life of the individual amoeba and the continued existence of the amoeba as a species. Another way of putting it is that *the utility of cognitive information* is attained when the action the subject has taken *brings about a change in the situational relationship between the subject and object,* enabling the subject to attain its goal. When a signal indicates to the amoeba the presence of food, the amoeba achieves the goal of selective action when it ingests the food. The situational relationship between the amoeba and the food changes, and the use of cognitive information, is a completed act.

The process, then, to realize the utility of cognitive information is structurally *the goal-oriented feedforward* of a subject itself, and the environment by the subject.

We are accustomed to the word 'feedback', which refers to *returning a deviation back within the control boundaries.* In 'feedforward', *a goal exists, but the boundaries of control are not fixed, and must be adjusted dynamically to a changing situational relationship.*

Usually, a subject must go through several information cycles to achieve the situational relationship and the use value of cognitive information that is its final goal. As each information cycle is completed, the subject achieves an intermediate level of utility, and a new situational relationship is established. The next signal the subject receives, thereby starting a new information cycle, stems from this new relationship. This process is repeated over and over until the subject achieves its final goal. The utility of cognitive information, therefore, is a result of a goal-oriented feedforward of a subject itself and its environment through the action of a subject to achieve a goal. Here goal-oriented feedforward is control in the direction of a goal. In response to changes in situational relations the subject controls its actions, and through its actions controls the external environment.

We can now give a more complete definition of 'cognitive information': it is *an informed situational relation between a subject and an object that makes possible the action selection by which the subject itself can achieve some sort of use value.*

This definition is sufficiently tenable as a general definition of information, if information is understood to be something counterposed to knowledge and technology.

'Knowlege' is no more than *cognitive information that has been generalized and abstracted from an understanding of the cause-and-effect relations of a particular phenomenon occurring in the external environment.* 'Technology' is *cognitive information that is useful in effectively carrying out production-oriented labor requiring a certain degree of prescribed expertise.* Fire-lighting technology in primitive society refers to production-oriented labor based on experience, such as 'rubbing wood together will light a fire.' Many repetitions of isolated instances of lighting a fire were necessary. In the beginning, empirical fire-lighting information was acquired by mere chance, and as information was accumulated from experience, it was passed on to others. Finally, standardized technological cognitive information became firmly established in human society, in what we know as technology.

Formation of Structurally Organic Information Networks

This is *the third* great characteristic of the information networks made possible by the combination of computers with communications technology. An *information network* is seen in the transmission of information between a large number of people within an extensive area made possible by the telephone and telegraph networks. This network, combined with a computer, has been developed into a network system that closely resembles information mechanisms as a living body, an organism.

A system of information in such a living body, the man-machine combination, can be broadly divided into two types of systems, *environmental* and *organismic*. These two systems of information are in a sense complementary sub-systems of information for the maintenance and development of the existing organism. Each has a different function.

The system of 'environmental information' is concerned with *the relation between an organism and the external world* in order to maintain its existence. The fundamental functions of the system of environmental information include such as to enable the organism to catch food and protect itself from enemies in order to survive. The system of 'organismic information' is concerned with carrying on *the essential functions within the living body* of the organism itself. The main function of the system of organismic information is to carry out physiological functions to maintain life within the body of the organism. The important point to note is that a primitive prototype of *the system of environmental information emerges from the highly developed system of organismic information.* Systems of organismic information are astonishingly intricate, yet are already wonderfully complete in protozoans. Be that as it may, what is important to stress here from the standpoint of the systems of information in organisms is that the existence of the intricate system of organismic information first made it possible for the system of environmental information to come into being.

Comparing the systems of organismic information in protozoans with the systems of environmental information in mankind that have come into being with computer technology reveals a number of similarities. *The first* is that both have *a memory function.* The protozoan has DNA that serves this function, and the computer has magnetic tapes and drums. In the protozoan the genetic code is inherited. There was no such thing as memory information until cognitive brains evolved in mammals. In this respect the computer is far ahead of the protozoan.

The second similarity is that both have *a programmatic function.* Common to both the protozoan and the computer is that they are provided with a program, and cannot produce it themselves. What is different is that while the protozoan's program is hereditarily fixed in the DNA as a genetic code, man creates a program for the computer for each time of usage.

The third similarity is that both have *a copy function.* In the protozoan a genetic code is copied from DNA onto RNA. In the computer, programs and data can be copied from the magnetic memory onto the CPU (central processing unit) of the computer.

The fourth similarity is that both have *a coding function.* In protozoans, the genetic code is retained in the form of unique genetic signals that indicate each of the characteristics of the four nucleotide bases (adenine, guanine, thymine, and cytosine) the component molecules of proteins and enzymes. A sequence of three nucleotide bases on an m-RNA strand (called a 'codon') indicate the amino acids that make up proteins and enzymes, and these are translated from m-RNA by t-RNA. In the computer, numbers and letters are coded into combinations of 0 1 bits, the information is processed in this state, and then these bit codes are translated back again into numbers and letters as output.

The fifth similarity is that both have *a control function—* discrimination, evaluation, and command. In the protozoan, RNA (a compound enzyme) has this function. The t-RNA discriminates between the amino acids in the food taken in, according to the combination of genetic signals that the t-RNA of the protozoan has copied, and brings each of these amino acids together according to a program. In this process the functions of discrimination, judgement, and evaluation are clear. Also, t-RNA is equipped with the coded signals 'start' and 'stop' in the program.

In the same way, the computer discriminates between and judges the information it has recognized. Based upon this, it can give instructions and control commands. It also signals 'start' and 'stop'.

Looked at this way, the system of environmental information that constitutes the information structure of the computer has begun strongly to resemble the system of organismic information. When the computer is joined with communications technology, the system of environmental information approaches the systems of organismic information of more sophisticated organisms, seen in three ways.

The first is the development of *the system of information transmission and control.* Similar to animals, which have a control system of motor and autonomic nerves extending throughout the body, the computer, with its communications lines, constitutes a cognitive information network, and makes possible networks of simultaneous concentration and dispersal of cognitive information. Data from many places can not only be concentrated and processed in one place, it can be simultaneously dispersed to many places.

Moreover, response networks came into being. Simultaneous concentration and dispersal of information processing began to be carried out continuously to provide instantaneous responses, and complex feedforward networks became the most sophisticated function of cognitive information networks. It became possible not only to present goal-directed feedforward continuously, but also to process and transmit many different types of feedforward information in a complex way.

The second similarity is *the development of diverse information organs.* In animals, information organs such as eyes, ears, mouth and nose are developed; in computer information networks, many different kinds of input and output apparatuses (line printers, cathode ray tubes, facsimile, intelligent terminals) are the terminal equipment.

The third similarity is *the development of advanced information processing technology.* In a human being, even a seemingly simple action like walking first becomes possible when there is information exchanged within a network of bodily organs, including, of course, the eyes, muscles of the legs, and the equilibrium organs of the middle ear. For computer networks there are also sophisticated means of information processing. On-line real time systems provide instantaneous response over long distances. Through time-sharing systems many people can use the computer at the same time. Teleconferencing uses television and the computer network to carry out conferences, without people having to assemble in one place. The remote sensing technology that resulted from joining the computer and communication satellites is a system of searching for weather conditions and resources allocation on a worldwide scale.

Possibility of Highly Organismic Society. The similarity of the system of environmental information of computer-communications technology to the system of organismic information in organisms suggests something important for the outlook of the future information society. The hypothesis can be formulated that the future information society will be a 'highly organismic society' resembling an organism. What I am referring to will probably be *a multicentered complex society* in which many systems are linked and integrated by information networks. Moreover, this society will have the dynamism to respond more quickly and more appropriately than contemporary society to changes in the external environment, and then the information society of the future will appear before us as a society with highly organic information space linked by a network of cognitive information with complex feedforward loops.

B. The Societal Impact of the Information Epoch

The information epoch to be brought about by computer-communications technology does not mean simply that it will have a big socio-economic impact upon contemporary industrial society; it will demonstrate a force of societal change powerful enough to bring about the transformation of society into a completely new type of human society, which is the information society.

Generally speaking, innovational technology changes social and economic systems through the following three stages:

Stage 1—in which technology does work previously done by man.
Stage 2—in which technology makes possible work that man has never been able to do before.
Stage 3—in which the existing social and economic structures are transformed into new social and economic systems.

The three stages of technological innovation, as they apply to the revolution in computer and communications technology, may be defined as *replacement and amplification of the mental labor of man and the transformation of human society.*
This may be defined as follows:

The first stage is *automation,* in which man's mental labor is includingly accomplished through the application of computer-communications technology.

The second stage is that of *knowledge creation,* which entails the amplification of man's mental labor.

The third stage is that of *system innovation,* a set of political, social and economic transformations resulting from the impact of the first two developmental stages.

A brief outline of the societal impact of the computer-communications revolution is shown in Fig. 5.3.[13]

Automation: The Replacement of Man's Mental Labor

Automation has traditionally been understood to involve the assumption of various kinds of mental activities (recognition, understanding, computation, memory, judgment, control, etc.) by computers or computer-driven servo-mechanisms. However, the expanding applications of computer-communications technology are changing this traditional concept to the extent that the future prospect for computer-oriented automation has greater potentialities than we commonly accept today.

First; computer-communications technology will bring about the complete automation of production. Industrial production is simply the process of applying scientific laws to change raw materials into useful goods, and the computer functions to feedback the production process quickly in response to such changes that occur during the production process. Computer automation began with evaluation and control, and went on to group control systems and the complete automation of a whole production process. In the near future, complete automation of entire plants will come into being, and during the next twenty or thirty years there will probably emerge, in fields related to energy and materials (electric power generation, oil refining, iron, cement, etc.), factories that require no manual labor at all.

Second; computer-communications technology will bring about *automation of knowledge-oriented services and operations.* Whenever man's knowledge-oriented activity is carried out in a fixed logical order, a computer can be programmed to perform in the same way. In knowledge-oriented services, many kinds of automated service machines, such as vending machines and cash dispensers, are already replacing the service labor of man. Even in medical treatment, automatic diagnosis devices, as used for examining patients suffering from cardiovascular ailments, have already been developed. In knowledge-oriented operations, clerical duties related to billing and accounting have already been completely replaced by the computer.

Third is *systems automation.* This is the automation that creates unified systems that combine many sub-automation functions organically in place of separate and independent feedback and control. The group numerical control systems of industrial production are typical examples of systems automation. Systems automation makes possible large scale integrated traffic control systems to optimize the flow of traffic through hundreds of intersections. Systems like the lunar landing system using satellites to put man on the moon, of course, are semi-automatic man-machine systems that

Fig. 5.3 Computer-Communications Revolution and Its Societal Impact

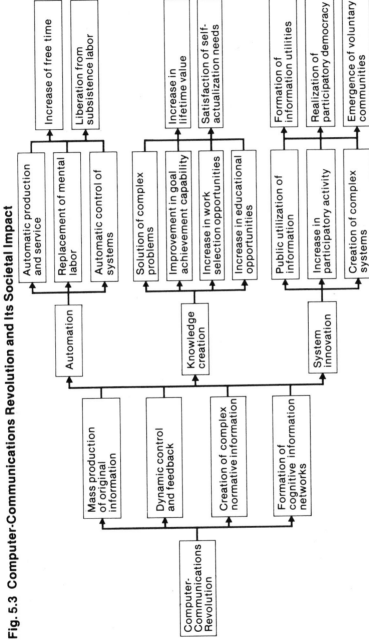

utilize computer-communications technology more than any other.

In discussing the social impact of automation, however, it is necessary to deal with the existence of both bright and dark potentials.

A first principal social impact will be *the increasing emancipation of man from labor for subsistence*: this will have an immeasurable social and psychological effect on the future of mankind, a social impact which may be said to belong to the bright side of automation. Ever since man's appearance on earth he has devoted the great bulk of his time to work merely to assure his physical survival. In this, man has been bound in space; that is, to the physical places of production. In the agricultural age, man was bound to earth, and in the industrial age, workers were virtually confined to factories and office workers to their offices. However, since a large portion of office and production work will be replaced by computers, there will be less need for men and women to serve as the medium of information storage and communication, which is, after all, the principal reason for human involvement in much organized work. Thus, man will not only be emancipated from the necessity to labor for subsistence, but he will also be freed from the bonds which have tied him to the places of production. Moreover, man will increasingly have more time to expend on his personal satisfactions.

In the light of these changing circumstances, it would be unreasonable to assume that the traditional concept of leisure will continue unchanged in an information society. It would be more reasonable to suppose that a new concept, suitable to the information epoch, will take the place of labor for subsistence. In this context, I prefer to refer to 'leisure' in the information age as 'free time.' Free time is not merely the opposite of work time; rather it is all time which may be disposed of freely by each individual. *Free time* may therefore be broken down into three parts:

The first is leisure in the conventional meaning of the word, the content of which is *rest* and *play*. But rest and play will not be able to fill our ample free time in the future.

The second part of free time would involve learning in the broadest meaning of the word. In other words, more and more people will spend their free time by studying systems sciences and computers in order to adapt themselves to the information epoch, or by taking lessons in cultural accomplishments, hobbies, arts, and crafts. (In the United States, adult schooling is already the fastest growing form of education.)

The third segment of free time will involve preparation for a better life in society, or for collecting and analyzing information for social activity and for working on plans for the future, and making projections.

If the freeing of man from subsistence labor is a positive social result of the information revolution, *a second* social result, *unemployment,* will represent a negative side of automation. There is ample reason to fear that the unemployment of old and middle-aged persons and the obsolescence of old techniques as a result of automation will pose a serious social problem. This is an unavoidable choice between either an increase in free time or mass unemployment, a choice that the future information society will have to face. I feel that, just as in the past, developments in industrial productive power have ultimately brought about an increase in consumption and income, not an increase in unemployment, the fruit of automation resulting from the development of information productive power in the near future will probably be an increase in free time, rather than unemployment.

A third social impact of automation is that of *social restraint.* This not only represents the darkest side of automation, but is also perhaps the most critical issue of applied computer-communications technology. While liberating us from labor for subsistence and providing us with ample free time, automation will bring the possibility of *invisible social restraint,* so called because it would not entail surveillance by secret police.

One such source of alienation would be related to man's restraint by functions or systems. As we have noted, automation will liberate us from the place of production and restrictions in time. Businessmen, for example, will be freed from the need to use packed commuter trains; their independent initiative will fill a higher role in their work. On the other hand, they will be more strictly subjected to management goals based on merit and performance. Further, management information systems (MIS) will relate each person's activities closely through various functions of management, and on-line, real-time control systems will establish very strict time schedules for these functional relationships. When such automatic management control systems become commonplace, functional and systematic restraints will replace the restrictions of place and time.

Another type of alienation will center upon the potential for *the invasion of privacy.* In an advanced information society, there will be thousands of data banks of various kinds which will contain massive information data on individuals and enterprises. For instance, a government social data bank will accumulate information according to a unified numbering system on all individuals with respect to their numerous activities from the cradle to the grave, while financial institutions will have detailed information on the balance sheets of every family. The use of such private data by government or by any other group of persons for a particular purpose would constitute a serious cause for the further alienation of man. Of course, laws will have to be formulated to prevent such invasions of privacy, but such laws could prove inadequate for the purpose.

Further alienation may result from the use of computer-communications technology to create *a managed society.* The managed society would operate in such a way that ruling elites would guide the 'managed' (persons and things), using information networks as control mechanisms. Information created by computers is confined to quantifiable and logical information; thus, much information regarding human aspects of life cannot be computerized. It therefore follows that a computer-managed society may become inhuman, or alienated from humanity. A completely automated state would be an intellectual ice age, devoid of humanity, in which a handful of data manipulators would dominate as an intellectual elite.

While recognizing these dangers, however, I believe that mankind will be able to avoid such a managed society, and be able to proceed to the second stage of development: knowledge creation. My reasons for confidence are taken up later.

Knowledge Creation: The Amplification of Man's Intellectual Labor

If automation entails the supplanting of man's mental labor by computer-communications technology, then *knowledge creation* is a concrete example of the amplification of mental labor through such technology.

By 'knowledge creation' is meant *the creation of intellectual values,* but this is only a commonplace and general definition, and is illusory. We can grasp it by seeing its two aspects; viz., *problem solving* and *opportunity development.* In this context, 'problem solving' is devising *a method or means of eliminating risks that may stand in the way of accomplishing an aim.* Computer-communications technology can help us expand our problem solving capacity by reaching beyond the limitations of time and space, a capacity found in the very technological foundations of computers—large memory capacity, high-speed calculation, integrated control functions—in an on-line, real-time system.

One of the most advanced problem-solving systems of this kind is the forecasting, evaluating and warning system, a system for quick discovery of problems in rapidly changing circumstances, forecasting a future trend, evaluating the degree of danger due to these problems, and issuing a warning when danger appears.

Problem solving systems of this type have some fundamental characteristics.

The first is that they are *pro-active*: a system for detecting a problem before it becomes serious, and by predicting future trends, projecting potential alternative solutions. *The second* is for discovering hitherto unknown problems. *The third* characteristic is that the problems to be solved by systems of this kind are very complex, protracted, and not straightforward (e.g. environmental disruption by chemicals).

Among large-scale forecasting, evaluating and warning functions the system is certain to provide in the future information society is ecological forecasting, evaluating and warning. Vast numbers of measuring instruments will be installed in all parts of the globe, from the Arctic to the Antarctic, to be used in conjunction with space observation satellites, all of which will be connected to regional centers. The regional centers will be connected to a United Nations center, where a computer, many times larger in capacity than conventional computers, will operate for this global ecological system. The U.N. center will supply constant information on weather conditions, air, sea and river pollution in different regions of the world, and on the basis of the information received, forecasts and warnings will be issued.

Far from being unrealistic, the U.N. is already working on such a system, the major problem of which is not technical. To implement it fully calls for readiness and a cooperative attitude of U.N. member nations, and a change in their philosophical thinking on the future of humanity, and in their sense of values.

The second aspect of knowledge creation is *opportunity development*. By 'opportunity development' is meant *research and development of possibilities of future time usage or creating new values in rapidly changing environmental conditions.* Opportunity development is encouraged by the existence of the *information utility,* which will come into being when information becomes a public commodity, similar to water and electricity, which one can obtain as needed. This is the important societal orientation of computer-communications technology. *The first* societal impact of the information utility is *an increase in the opportunity for education.*

With the development of the information utility, one will be able to acquire and use cognitive information at any place and any time; this means that education will be freed from the restrictions of income, time and place. The result will be that all human beings will have the educational opportunities they desire, with conditions that make it possible for them to develop the full potentialities of the future.

The second impact will be *the increase in opportunities for work.* Through the information utility, people will be able to obtain much more information more quickly than now, relating to the possibilities for new work. People will have many opportunities for choice when selecting future work or the direction of their social activity. A new industry, *the opportunity industry,* will develop in response to the need of individuals and groups for opportunities for development. The opportunity industry will aim to help individuals and groups develop and realize their future potentials.

The main sectors of the opportunity industry will be the education industry, the information industry, the mass communication industry, and the consultation industry; and industries concerned with psychosomatic medicine and molecular biology, for example, will also have their part. There may even emerge something resembling religious activities, as we see religion in various forms again becoming a day-to-day factor in life in the 21st century.

System Innovation: Emergence of New Socio-Economic Systems

The third aspect of the information epoch will be *system innovation.* This means that present socio-economic systems will be replaced by new socio-economic systems. System innovation will be the most far-reaching effect of the information epoch.

When epoch-making technological innovation occurs, changes take place in the existing society and a new society emerges. The steam engine precipitated the industrial revolution, bringing about changes that led to a new economic and political system: the capitalist system and parliamentary democracy. The information epoch resulting from computer-communications technology will bring about a societal transformation just as great or even greater than the industrial revolution.

Let us look at some typical examples of major and basic transformations to be expected: a change in our values system from material to time value; from a system of free competition to a synergetic economic system; from parliamentary democracy to participatory democracy.

These matters are discussed in detail later; let us focus on the transformation in the educational system, as a most dramatic societal change.

The first change will be *to lift education out of the restrictions of formal schools.* The present closed educational environment will be replaced by an open educational environment, made up of *knowledge networks.* It will eradicate the educational gaps between town and countryside, and between industrial and non-industrialized countries.

The second change will be *the introduction of a personal type of education,* suited to the ability of each individual, replacing the traditional uniform system of collective education with a system determined by individual ability and choice. This will become possible through educational programs suited to different levels of scholastic attainment with a wide range of educational opportunities. This means that the present educational system, graded according to age, will be supplanted by a system that allows the people's abilities to move on to advanced courses, irrespective of age, and where even children of lesser ability will be able to improve their levels of learning by means of personal-type lessons and guidance.

Thirdly, the system of self-learning will become the leading form of education. The formal educational system has been one of unilateral teaching of students by teachers. When a system of self-learning is introduced, teachers will act as advisers or counsellors. This will be possible because, as a result of the development and spread of CAI (computer-aided instruction) systems, students will be able to study by themselves, watching CRT displays and conversing with a computer and with other people by computer.

The fourth change will be to *knowledge-creative education.* Education in this industrial society aims at cramming the heads of students with bits of information and training them in techniques. This will be replaced with knowledge-creative education and training, because the information society will develop through information values into a high knowledge-creation society.

The fifth change will mean *lifetime education.* The present education system is centered on compulsory education to be completed when young. There are few higher and professional opportunities of learning available to the average person after that. In the information society, however, greater importance will be attached to the education of adults and even older people, because this will be necessary to enable adults and elderly people to adapt themselves to the changes of the information society. and to develop their abilities for society as a whole to accept the increasing proportion of elderly people in the population.

This radical change in the educational system will be of great significance to the development of human history—a historical transition from industrial society, in which the natural environment has been unilaterally transformed and material consumption expanded, to the information society which seeks coexistence with nature through mankind's own transformation and innovation of new socio-economic systems.

6
Globalism: The Spirit of a Neo-Renaissance

Past history reveals that a new spirit has always supplanted the old when society has begun to disintegrate and the emergence of new society has begun. For example when feudalistic agricultural society, which had lasted for many hundreds of years, began to break up, and industrial society began to emerge, and the renaissance spirit became the new spirit of the times.

The New Spirit of the Times

What will be the spirit of the times? What will be the concept characterizing the thought of the times in the information society? It will be *globalism*. This will actually signify a neo-renaissance in the sense that it will emerge in the passing of the old society, which gives place to the new society (industrial society to information society), the chief aim of which will be the liberation of the human spirit. The character and content of this neo-renaissance will differ fundamentally from the earlier renaissance in two ways:

The first characteristic of globalism is what we may call *space-ship thought*. [14] If we term the renaissance an era of explosion, the neo-renaissance is an era of implosion. The old territorial frontiers that divide mankind are breaking down, a fact graphically illustrated by the shortage of natural resources. Particularly noteworthy is the growing shortage of fossil fuels and metals, such as petroleum, copper, lead etc. We recognize this as a real problem, the emergence of an entirely new situation since the Industrial Revolution, in which, even if industrial productivity is raised and material wants are increased, industrial production will sooner or later level off because of shortages of raw materials.

Man succeeded in making a soft-landing on the moon, but tens of thousands of people cannot be settled on the moon, though this was possible in settling the American continent. Mankind has no alternative but for the 4,000 million earth people to fulfil their destiny on this closed planet called earth. Herein we find the historical background to the spaceship thought.

The second characteristic is *the idea of symbiosis.* This is the concept of peaceful symbiosis, the symbiosis of mankind and nature, a new thought of our time, prevailing over liberalism and individualism. The historical background to this is the development of the ultimate sciences, along with the pollution problems that have arisen. The first ultimate science is nuclear science. The development of nuclear energy, which threatened to exterminate mankind in a thermonuclear war, led to the peaceful coexistence system between the United States and the Soviet Union, predominating over ideological differences, and placing curbs on nuclear weapons. The subsequent developments of ultimate biological sciences, including the conversion of chromosomes and artificial impregnation, make it urgent that a new view of ethics be established, particularly affecting the ultimate problem of life.

The essence of the pollution problems is in the enormous industrial productivity made possible by the application of science and technology to mass production, and the emergence of a society of high mass consumption. The consequent discharge of enormous quantities of industrial and consumption wastes is seriously harming nature and causing environmental disruption, so that now a serious danger threatens the normal life and health of human beings. The appearance of pollution and the damage to nature led to the new science of ecology, from which the idea of the symbiosis of nature and man arises.

The third characteristic is the concept of *global information space* (GIS). As distinct from conventional geographical space, this means space connected by information networks. It is space without regional boundaries. When this information space is expanded to global proportions, it will be global information space, formed on the basis of a global information infrastructure of communication lines, communication satellites and linked-up computers.

Information has *no national boundaries.* When global information space is formed, world-wide communication activities among citizens that cross all national boundaries will be set in motion, and as mutual exchanges of information expand, so will mutual understanding deepen, touching problems that lie outside the boundaries of nations and states (eg., the population explosion and energy problems), making it possible to deal with these problems from the global standpoint. When this happens, the spirit of globalism, prevailing over conflicting national interests and differences, will become broadly and deeply rooted in the minds of the people.

7
Time-Value: A New Concept of Value

What Is Time-Value?

This new concept of value will come with the future information society, for time value will be the major determinant of modes of action.

'Time value' is[15] *the value which man creates in the purposeful use of future time.* Put in more picturesque terms, *man designs a goal on the invisible canvas of his future, and goes on to attain it.* As we have said, time is an intangible, abstract concept, by which we mean the measurement of the passage of time. But if conceived of as a person's lifetime, time used for the satisfaction of wants, time itself creates value.

The development of information productivity through computer communications technology has given rise to a new basic concept of time-value to replace material values. The relations between information productivity and time-value are set out below, showing how the development of information productivity produces time-value.

The first point is *the increased effectiveness of purposeful action.* Computer-communications technology makes it possible to mass-produce foreseeing, logical and action-selective information. As a result, the effectiveness of purposeful action is greatly increased.

This change in the pattern of action necessarily tends to place more importance on time-value, or the effective utilization of time.

The second point is *the importance attached to time as a necessary ingredient of a compound process.* Knowledge-oriented information created by computer-communications technology has the character of compound and normative information. Such information eliminates much of the limitation on the scale and time of purposeful action, and so the process becomes an important factor in producing time-value. 'Process' means here the *interaction of a purposeful subject on the field or in the compound space in which the subject acts.*

The third point is *the increase of free time.* Computer-communications technology greatly increases automation functions in material
production. The replacement of man's feedback functions in
material production promotes automation in material production,
and liberates man from the restraint on time for material production,
and so increases free time.

For these three reasons, a substantial improvement in information
productivity through computer-communications technology makes
it possible to create new time value to replace the conventional
material value.

The Framework of Time-Value

The value, as seen from the standpoint of a value system, comes
within a triple framework; subject of action, field, and process. The
reason why these difficult concepts—subject of action, field, and
process—are introduced here is that the concept of time-value
becomes clear only when seen within this triple framework.

As for 'the subject of action,' i.e. *the subject which works on
the field with objective-consciousness,* this may be any individual,
group of individuals, or organizations engaging in social action with
deliberate purpose; an individual, enterprise, nonprofit organization,
local autonomous entity, government, state, a consumer movement,
or a group of people engaged in a citizens' movement.

As for the concept of 'field', this is *the space, with concrete
content, within which the subject of action acts with conscious
purpose.* However, the field in this case is not an objectively pre-
existing field, but is necessarily related to the working of the subject
of action and also to reality.

Another new concept of field is the field of *information space.*
This is the field provided within the new space, which had never
previously existed and which is connected with the networks of
information. This field of information space is characterized by
two features: 1) it does *not have boundaries* like a territorial field
and 2) in this field, *elements related by objective-oriented action are
related to each other through information networks.* The concept of
field in information-oriented society will be represented more and
more by this concept of information space. (See Fig. 7.1)

As for the third concept, 'process', this is *the development in
time of a situation created artifically by the interaction between the
purposeful action on the field of the subject of action and the
reaction of the field to it,* and regarded as the dynamic process of
a system comprising both the subject of action and the field. By

Fig. 7.1 Two Types of Fields

A. Field of Geographical Space **B. Field of Information Space**

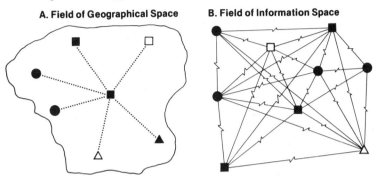

the artificially created situation is meant a situation purposefully created by the objective-oriented action of the subject of action so that the objective may be attained.

Further, this process is characterized by the fact that it is finally completed. This is because the subject of action puts an end to the action when the purpose is either attained or given up.

The result of any achievement produced in the triple framework—the subject of action, field, and the process—is precisely time-value, which is measured according to the degree and quality of the results achieved. Further, time value may be the situation itself in which the process ends, or it may be the sum total of the value produced during the process, depending on the value judgment of the subject of action.

In this outline of the framework of time-value, the relationship between subject, field, and process may become clearer by looking

Fig. 7.2 Value System of Time-value

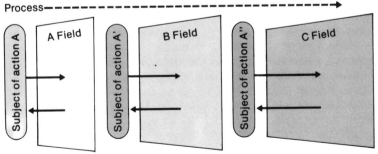

Time-value means value created by the expenditure of free time in an objective-oriented way.

at Figure 7.2. The subject of action acts on the field. Through this action, Field A, changing, shifts into Field B, which in turn, changing, shifts into Field C. The situational relationship, including both the subject of action and the field, goes on changing, shifting, and developing continuously. Time-value is produced in this changing and developing process.

This time-value is on a higher plane in human life than material values as the basic value of economic activity. This is because time-value corresponds to the satisfaction of human and intellectual wants, whereas material value corresponds to the satisfaction of physiological and material wants. If we define physiological and instructive wants as primary, the desire to satisfy oneself through purposeful action may be called a secondary want.

In conclusion, it may be said that the increase in productivity of knowledge-oriented information is the only motivating force that can directly heighten time-value.

8
The Information Utility: Societal Symbol of the Information Society

While industrial society is a society formed and developed around the production of material values, the information society will be formed and developed around the production of information values. In industrial society the modern factory is a large machinery production facility which has the central function in the production of goods. This modern factory, the present societal symbol, supplanted the farm, which had been the main base of production in agricultural society. In the information society of the future the *information utility* will become the base of production of information values, and thus could appropriately be called the societal symbol of the information society.[16]

What Is an Information Utility?

An 'information utility' is *an information infrastructure* consisting of public information processing and service facilities that combine computer and communication networks. From these facilities *anyone, anywhere, at any time will be able easily, quickly, and inexpensively to get any information which one wants to get.*

The following four requirements will be essential to an information utility.

1. Central facilities equipped with large scale computers capable of simultaneous parallel processing, connected with large capacity memory devices, a large number of program packages and extensive data bases. Such facilities will be able to do information processing and provide services for a large number of users at the same time.
2. Such information process and service facilities will be provided for the use of the general public, for which purpose the computers of the central facilities will be connected by means of a communi-

cations circuit directly to terminals in businesses, schools, and homes.

3. Any user will be able to call the local center of the information utility to have data processed, or one will even be able to process the necessary data for oneself.

4. The cost of using the services of the center must be low to enable the general public to use the center readily for day-to-day needs.

There is a system already in existence which partly meets these conditions. It can be seen in the commercial time-sharing service and the utilization of computer networks operating between universities. But these systems are restricted to certain social strata (large enterprises and universities), and the costs are high. It was once thought that it would be several decades before information utilities could become available to meet all these conditions fully, but the development of ICs (integrated circuits) in the early 1970s ushered in the era of full-fledged information utilities.

There are at present two main currents in the world to support this claim. One is the experiments on community information systems, such as the Tama CCIS and Hi-Ovis of Japan and Sweden's Project TERESE (see Chapters 1 and 2, Part I), and the other is the development and practical application of the *video data systems,* including those of the United Kingdom (Prestel), West-Germany, the United States, Canada (TELIDON) and Japan (CAPTAINS).

Video-data systems allow users telephone access on demand to information stored in computers, which is then displayed for them on modified television sets. The system uses span publishing, marketing, in-house communication, public service information, education and entertainment.

These systems have the ideal features required for an information utility, including (1) they supply diversified information, (2) they require only a small investment ($300–$500), (3) service charges are as low as telephone charges (10–20 cents per operation), (4) they are easy to operate (select push-button system). These factors open up the possibility of tens of millions of sets being installed throughout the world, even by the 1980s. The advent of full-fledged information utilities can be considered now to be on the horizon.

Can we now project the picture of a future information utility as the societal symbol of the information society?

A desirable and feasible future information utility will represent the integration of three concepts—(1) information infrastructure, (2) joint production and shared utilization, and (3) citizen participation.

Formation of Information Infrastructure

The first fundamental of the information utility as we conceive it is that *it will take the form of an information infrastructure.*

There are two reasons for saying this. *First,* the information utility will be required to have all that is essential to the other parts of the infrastructure, including electricity, water, railroads, etc. The information utility will (1) become indispensable to the support, development and maintenance of socio-economic activity, (2) require massive investments in equipment and facilities, (3) be linked in a regional and/or nationwide network. Information utilities will share all three conditions with the existing components of the infrastructure.

Second, the information utility by its very nature will be for the use and benefit of the public, its service being of a unique character, that is *self-multiplication.* In the first place, information, unlike material goods, has four inherent properties that have made self-multiplication possible.

1. It is *not consumable*— goods are consumed in being used, but information remains however much it is used.
2. It is *non-transferable*—in the transfer of goods from A to B, they are physically moved from A to B, but in the transfer of information it remains with A.
3. *Indivisible*—materials such as electricity and water are divided for use, but information can be used only as 'a set'.
4. *Accumulative*—the accumulation of goods is by their non-use, but information cannot be consumed or transferred, so it is accumulated to be used repeatedly. The quality of information is raised by adding new information to what has already been accumulated.

Synergetic Production and Shared Utilization of Information

The second fundamental is that both *the production and utilization will be a combined operation.* This means that the production structure of information is *self-multiplying.*

'Self-multiplication' does not mean the successive production of new information, but *the utility's continuous expansion in the production of information, both in quantity accumulation and qualitative improvement.* All information produced by the information utility is cumulative, with new information constantly being added. In simpler terms, *the accumulation of information leads to further accumulation of information which in turn means still further accumulation of information over time and space.* One can say that information utilities are systems that demonstrate to the maximum the self-multiplication function of information by man-machine methods.

There will be four stages of development by which the man-machine self-multiplication production systems of information utilities will come to maturation, viz., 1) public services, 2) user production, 3) shared utilization, 4) synergetic production and utilization.

Stage 1—*Public Services Stage:* This is the stage at which the information utility provides information processing and services for the public. Many kinds of programs and data bases are prepared by the utilities in advance, and users utilize the information service within the limits of this preparatory stage. (Videodata systems belong in this stage).

Stage 2—*User Production Stage*: At this stage, the user of the information utility produces information. The user collects data, makes the program, and makes use of the information utility to produce the user's own required information. There are four factors to promote user-production of information; *the first* being the awareness of the general public that one's own information can be produced for oneself. *The second* will be the development of sophisticated language programs in the conversational mode. *The third* will be the development of various packaged program modules, and *the fourth* will be the preparation of data bases to suit many different fields. These factors will enable the general public to become aware of their ability to produce and the value of producing their own information.

Stage 3—*Shared Utilization Stage:* At this stage, the information utility makes possible the shared use of information produced by individual users. As the production of separate information by individuals reaches a certain point, the data and programs are registered and become available to third parties, and the self-multiplication process and shared utilization interact to produce a geometric effect.

Stage 4—*Synergetic Production and Shared Utilization Stage:* The synergetic production of information by a group belongs to this stage. The shared use of information by the voluntary registration of programs and data developed by individuals develops into voluntary synergetic production and shared utilization of information by groups. It is evident that several people working together in collecting and processing data will be more efficient. There will be frequent need for complex programs that will only be possible when several people work together in the development and utilization of the product. This is obviously so in the development and shared utilization of complex technology and programming to resolve the more complex problems.

Synergetic production and shared utilization of information will be the most developed form of information production by the self-multiplying operation of the information utility.

Three Types of Information Utility

The third fundamental is *citizen participation*. Three possible types of management can be envisaged for the information utility: the business, government managed and the citizen managed types.

In the long run, the citizen oriented mixed type will probably become predominant because citizen participation will be essential to the management of information utilities. This becomes clear if one looks at the shape that these three types of management can assume, and then notes, from a macro point of view, the socio-economic merits and demerits of each.

A. The Business Type

The business type of information utility will be privately capitalized, and its functions will be exercised on a wholly commercial basis by free competition of private enterprise. Operations will be based on the income to be derived from information processing and services. The major types of services will be information such as is related to every-day convenience in the lives of the general public (news requests, information on shopping, etc.), or concerned with various sorts of mental exercises or recreation (spaceship games).

Chief merits of the business type are that efficiency in management will be essential and the services thorough. Negative values would result from excessive commercialism resulting in information services encouraging mental laziness and stagnation by the emphasis placed on convenience, accompanied by aggressive advertising.

B. Government Type

The capital required for the governmentally managed information utility would be provided from the national budget, the goal of which would be to increase the well-being of the people as a whole. The national government would operate the utilities, with the dual support of taxes and revenue from the utility rates in payment for services. The services would include all forms of public relations, information about government policy, statistics, information to serve the public interest (weather, pollution, transportation, etc.), and information services of a social welfare nature, such as education and medical care.

The chief merits would be the low rates for usage and the requirement that such utilities exist for the public good. Negative values would derive from the inefficiency associated with bureaucratic organization and the danger of increased governmental control over society.

C. Citizen Management Type

Here, a third type of capital is civils, differing from private capital, raised by citizens themselves. Operations would be completely under *the autonomous management of the citizens,* with the operational base consisting of *funds raised by citizens,* from usage fees, and *voluntary contributions* (these would include money, mental labor, and programming).

Both the processing and supplying of information will be essentially in the form of joint production and shared utilization by the citizens themselves, with types of information related to problem solving, opportunity development for individuals, groups, and even society as a whole.

Here, the merits will be maximum of voluntary participation of citizens, allowing the individual to obtain the information needed. It becomes so much easier to arrive at a solution and the direction for joint action to solve common social problems. A demerit is that in capital formation, technology, and organization, this type is inferior to the previous two because functionally it would depend to a very great extent on the voluntary contributions of citizens, which would be difficult to coordinate.

The three types of management for the information utility have here been stereotyped and somewhat exaggerated as to the characteristics of each. Considered realistically, the information utility of the future is likely to be a combination of two or three types.

Citizen Participation Is Essential

Whatever the combination, citizen participation is an essential condition, the most desirable form of which would be mixed and

Table 8.1 Three Types of Information Utilities

	Business Type	Government Managed Type	Citizen Managed Type
Management Goal	Profit	Welfare	Information accumulation
Type of Capital	Private capital	Government capital	Civil capital
Type of Management	Private	Government	Autonomous
Form of Production	Time sharing services	Data banks	Synergetic production
Area of Service	Daily convenience, leisure	Medical care, education	Problem solving, opportunity développements
Operations Base	Sales revenue	Usage rates, taxes	Voluntary contributions, usage rates
Price System	Free price system	Public utility rate system	Income standard system
Merits	Efficient, good service	Operated in the public interest, inexpensive	Autonomous, creative
Demerits	Commercialism, mental degeneration	Danger of control, inefficiency	Weak, unstructured operations base

citizen-oriented. The main reason is that (1) only by citizen participation in the management of information utilities will the self-multiplicative production effect of information be expanded, (2) autonomous group decision making by ordinary citizens will be promoted, and (3) the dangerous tendency toward a centralized administrative society will be prevented.

The Macro-Cummulative Effect of Information. *The first* reason why information utilities will tend toward citizen management is that this type of information utility, more than any other, will facilitate the macro-cumulative effect of information. I have already mentioned that self-multiplication of information production gives the information utility the nature of an information infrastructure. When viewed from the perspective of the national economy, the self-multiplication can be called *the macro cumulative effect* of information; the effect being in sharp contrast to *the mass production effect* of goods produced in the modern factories of industrial society.

In the production of goods, the expansion in manufacturing that follows a big increase in production equipment has a great mass production effect. That is to say, the greater the investment in capital equipment, the more productive power increases and production costs decrease. This decrease in costs expands the market and encourages further profits and further accumulation of capital. This mass production effect of goods is, from the enterprise's point of view, the multiplying effect of capital, in the sense that any accumulation of capital results in further accumulation of capital.

The self-multiplication of private capital has been a fundamental cause of the formation and expansion of modern manufacturing industries as a whole.

In the case of information also, expansion in the scale of production cannot be ignored, but here the cumulative effect is more important.

The most important point in the production of information from a macro standpoint is *the self-multiplication of information value* itself—how to accumulate information and how to continue the further accumulation of information by adding new information to what has already been accumulated.

The information utility is not used simply by a limited group of users; it is widely used in the public interest by people in general. Moreover, it is the general public themselves that operate the information utility freely. Having the information utility take the form of synergetic production and shared use will raise the macro-cumulative effect of information utilities to the highest level. The citizen management type that is oriented toward voluntary synergistic production and shared use of information by citizens themselves is the form of management of the information utility that will have the greatest macro-cumulative effect, rather than the business type that aims to increase profits through the self-multiplication of capital, or the government managed type that prevents citizens from using the information utility freely.

Autonomous Group Decision Making. *The second* ground for confidence is that *this type makes autonomous group decision making possible*, with the aim of solving complex socio-economic problems through autonomous decisions by the citizens themselves.

The inadequacy of governmental compulsion and monetary compensation in solving the problems of human existence will stimulate these possibilities even further. The future information society will be a society in which autonomous decision making will be the most basic human right. The causes of problems that will arise in the future will be very complex and interrelated, and in complex opposition to these will be the individual group interests of the citizens. In solving such problems, *mutual understanding* and *voluntary cooperation* of each citizen in selecting the action that correspomds to one's own situation will be essential.

Avoiding a Controlled Society. *The third* reason is that only through this type can *the information society avoid the dangers of a controlled society.* For the information society to become an ideal society of voluntary decision making, and to avoid the ultimate fearful Orwellian automated state, will depend on the form of management adopted for the information utility.

If information utilities were to be completely dominated by a despotic state organization, the information society would be the ultimate controlled society, in which the abuses would by far exceed the alienation of man in the present industrial society or the abuse of human rights under dictatorships. This could occur because, in information utilities, both public and personal information concerning each individual is filed and accumulated, and, in addition, information about one's major activities in society would be added constantly to this file.

But if the information utilities are completely entrusted to the voluntary management of the citizenry, and if the personal information of individuals is completely protected and used to improve the private life of each individual and the quality of one's social activities, then the information utility will be of immeasurable benefit to all citizens. For example, the information utility will not simply provide the individual with information that is useful in solving everyday problems (illness, work, learning, housing, etc.) of the citizens, but will also contribute greatly to maintaining the individual's life in a healthy active state, by combining this sort of social information with personal data about each individual.

Looked at in this way, the information utility is a socio-economic institution which concentrates the ultimate in scientific technology. In this sense also *the autonomous management by citizens* of the information utility is an essential prerequisite for the ideal information society.

Vision of Global Information Utility

The information utility will extend to an international scale; it will reach a substantial level of development, and then will become a GIU (global information utitity).[17]

The concept of a GIU projects a global information infrastructure using a combination of computers, communication networks and satellites. Its basic feature would be that any ordinary citizen in the world could obtain all necessary information readily, quickly and at low cost, at any time and place in the world.

A GIU would operate on the following minimum requirements:

1. Several global information switching centers (GISCs) throughout the world, each of which would be connected to several scores of sub-global information utilities (sub-GIUs) would be required. Each sub-GIU would be equipped with a number of large capacity computers capable of on-line real-time processing of information.
2. GISCs would be mutually connected by satellites so that users could utilize not only sub-GIUs in their areas but also sub-GIUs in any place in the world through the GISCs.
3. Fees for GIUs services would need to be low enough for ordinary citizens in any country of the world to be able to use the facility on a day-by-day basis.
4. The basic computer language for GIUs should be an internationally standardized language, whereas input-output languages for individuals in different countries would have to be their native languages. For this purpose, each GIU would have to be equipped with an automatic translation system.

When GIUs come into practical application, it will be possible for people anywhere in the world, for instance, to call to their aid such services as CAI-oriented self-education systems, library and other information services, world news services, comparative studies of incomes and pensions with other countries, planning overseas travel for oneself, and competitive mental games according to time differences between different parts of the world. Imagine an international TV game contest. Thousands of different TV games will be possible, with contests among international mixed teams; GIU prizes can be awarded for the invention of new and exciting games. A computer art contest could be very colorful and artistic.

The following ideas would be of the greatest significance to mankind Take, for example, the accumulation of data on air-pollution at GIU's from time to time, gathered from many thousands of places in the world; this would become a global air-pollution information and correction system. The enormous volume of air-pollution information thus collected by GIU's would be at hardly any cost, by the voluntary cooperation of citizens in many countries.

Of more revolutionary significance would be *a global voting system*, by which hundreds of millions of people in the world would be able to participate in making decision, global problems—such as nuclear power generation and SSTs—which could have an unpredictable effect on the whole human race.

If such vision of GIUs were to become a reality, it would have an incalculable impact on human society.

1. As such exchanges of information among ordinary citizens in different countries of the world become a reality, a supra-national GIU system, overriding national interests, would be established as a result of increased cohesion of citizens.
2. The establishment of a global CAI education system would enable 90 per cent or more of the world's population to become literate, and a world language, distinct from Esperanto, would ultimately be developed.
3. The functioning of a global medical care and pollution prevention systems would eliminate leprosy, malaria and other endemic diseases, and lengthen the average life span of humans to 90 years or more. At the same time, birth control would be effectively practiced so that the total population of the world could be stabilized at 5,000 million or so.
4. The south-north gaps in wealth and cultural levels would be narrowed, and as values were diversified and individual and autonomous group activities were encouraged, a widened range of creative cultures would flourish.
5. A new society, with new economic principles, would come about, consistent with the basic characteristics of GIU's—the global joint creation and utilization of information. Thus, the transformation from the present individualistic principle of free competition to the principle of synergic activity among independent individuals cooperating functionally for a common objective would eventuate; human society formed on the principle of synergetic cooperation would mean a global society based on mutual assistance.

If what we have envisaged above is realized, GIUs can be expected to develop by geometric progression in the coming decade. This calls for preparations as listed below to be made as soon as possible to promote the formation of GIUs to meet these international needs.

1. Conclusion of *an international treaty on the joint control of communication satellites*
2. Establishment of *an international information development organ* to promote the establishment of GIUs,
3. Formulation of *concrete medical care and education projects for developing countries*

4. Promotion of *standardization of hardware and software related to GIUs*

9
A Synergetic Economic System:
An Information Axis Economy

In considering the economic structure in relation to the system of the information society, the information society will be a society that develops around the production of information values, as I have said, and will therefore differ fundamentally from the agricultural and industrial societies of the past, which developed around the production of material values. More precisely, the term information society refers to an economy in which (1) *information is the core of society's economic needs*, (2) *the economy, and society itself, grow and develop around this core, the production and use of information values,* and (3) *the importance of information as an economic product exceeds goods, energy, and services.* This economic structure could be called an 'information axis economy.'[18]

On the supposition that the information axis economy centering on the production of information comes into being, what changes will it bring about in the system and structure of the economy?

A. Change to an Information-Led Type of Industrial Structure

First, there will be *a change from an industrial structure centering around goods, energy, and services to an information-led type of industrial structure,* a change that will pass through three stages of development.

The Appearance of Information-Related Industries

The first stage will be *the formation of information-related industries.* In an information society the information-related industries will become the leading industries, which will develop to the point of formation of *quanternary industries* as a new classification.

The concept of 'quaternary industries' is necessary as a classification, in that a clear line of demarcation must be drawn between service industries and information-related industries. There is a general tendency to characterize the major change in the structure of post-industrial society as an expansion of tertiary industries (i.e. service industries) with their importance exceeding that of the secondary (manufacturing) industries. In this context, information-related industries could be classified as tertiary industries only because they are non-goods-producing industries. But it is highly probable that information-related industries would develop beyond the service industries in an information society. It is reasonable therefore to distinguish information-related industries from service industries, and classify them as quaternary industries, to provide a clear concept of the industrial structure of an information society.

What would be the composition of the quaternary industries, as leading industries of the future? Quaternary industries can be divided broadly into four main industrial groups: (1) information industries, (2) knowledge industries, (3) arts industries, and (4) ethics industries. Of these four, the information and the knowledge industries will become the key industries of the future. Figure 9.1 gives a breakdown of all information related industries.

The first 'information industries' will primarily be industries that produce, process, and service cognitive information, or produce and sell related equipment. Here, the information industries are restricted to cognitive information because a separate industrial group, the arts industries, will be established for affective information. The core of the information industries will comprise the information machinery industries, including the computer and peripheral equipment industries, and LSIs (large scale integrated circuits) and micro processors. Such information machinery industries will probably displace the automobile industry and take first place as the largest manufacturing industry.

Strictly speaking, one could classify these information machinery industries as secondary industries, but information-related industries are here given a broader meaning and come under the term 'quaternary industries.'

In parallel with this, the industries concerned with information processing services and systems development: software, TSS services, and computer centers, will also undergo unprecedented development. The present mass communications industry of newspapers and publishing, which dominate the information services, will probably enter an era of stagnation.

Fig. 9.1 The Quaternary Industries (Information-related Industries)

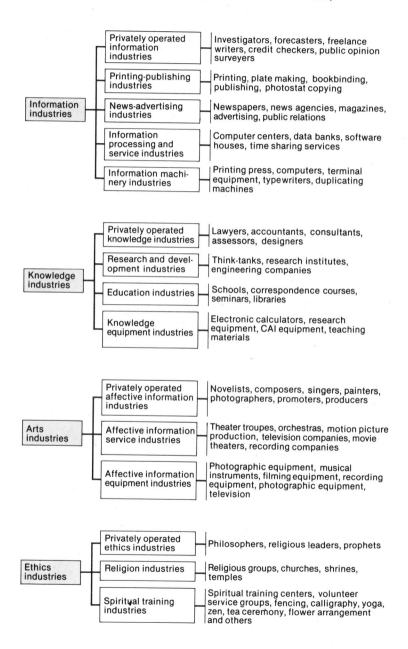

Information industries		
	Privately operated information industries	Investigators, forecasters, freelance writers, credit checkers, public opinion surveyors
	Printing-publishing industries	Printing, plate making, bookbinding, publishing, photostat copying
	News-advertising industries	Newspapers, news agencies, magazines, advertising, public relations
	Information processing and service industries	Computer centers, data banks, software houses, time sharing services
	Information machinery industries	Printing press, computers, terminal equipment, typewriters, duplicating machines

Knowledge industries		
	Privately operated knowledge industries	Lawyers, accountants, consultants, assessors, designers
	Research and development industries	Think-tanks, research institutes, engineering companies
	Education industries	Schools, correspondence courses, seminars, libraries
	Knowledge equipment industries	Electronic calculators, research equipment, CAI equipment, teaching materials

Arts industries		
	Privately operated affective information industries	Novelists, composers, singers, painters, photographers, promoters, producers
	Affective information service industries	Theater troupes, orchestras, motion picture production, television companies, movie theaters, recording companies
	Affective information equipment industries	Photographic equipment, musical instruments, filming equipment, recording equipment, photographic equipment, television

Ethics industries		
	Privately operated ethics industries	Philosophers, religious leaders, prophets
	Religion industries	Religious groups, churches, shrines, temples
	Spiritual training industries	Spiritual training centers, volunteer service groups, fencing, calligraphy, yoga, zen, tea ceremony, flower arrangement and others

The second group, the 'knowledge industries,' can be expected to develop after the information industries have come into being. The core of these will be of two types, viz., education industries and research and development industries. The education industries and the information industries together will be the pillars of the information society. The reason for this is that in the information society human values will change; material values will be superseded by time values, and greater importance will be attached to the development of new abilities and the improvement of human life. Research and development industries will greatly expand in response to the need to solve problems of resources and energy, an example of which would be resources recycling technology, or the need to improve human welfare through integrated social systems.

The third information-related industrial groups remain to be considered. The 'arts industries,' like the mass communication industries (newspapers, publishing, etc.) seem to have reached a peak now, and it is likely they will be declining industries. The reason is that in an information society the expansion of individual creative knowledge will flourish, and society will be able to escape from the present fad-oriented, sensory, television-dominated society of today. The future of television is probably that it will be linked with the computer and function more as a medium for cognitive information. One main use, for example, would be for citizen participation in decision-making on social problems.

The fourth group, the 'ethics industries,' by contrast, will become growth industries, among which religion will form a particularly important part. In this case, while moving away from belief in the existence of a supernatural god, religion will be epochally significant, in that human life will be elevated through renewed belief in the existence and strength of humanity. In the information society, on one hand, each person will attach more importance to scientific thought, and on the other, will be humble before an absolute existence that transcends human abilities. The very basis of this humility will be the global concept, the harmony and symbiosis of man and nature on this finite planet, earth. Whether one calls this globalism a religion or calls it the awareness of a supra-human existence, I believe the future will call for religious thought and an ethical content that are new and clothed in new attire.

In the information society of the future, these quaternary industries, and the computer industries, the information processing and service industries, the education industries, and the religion industries will together form a group of core industries whose major function will be in the growth and development of the quaternary industries as a whole.

The Formation of Industries with Installed Information Equipment

The second stage will be marked by *the formation of industries with installed information equipment.* This means the informationalization of industries through utilization of the machinery, with information equipment forming part of it. The development of machinery and equipment capable of exercising information functions has been made possible through the invention of LSIs and microprocessors. We have already reached the stage where a wide range of machinery with installed information equipment, such as electronic calculators, electronic watches (digital or other), automatic cameras, cash dispensers, games machines, etc. are on the market. In the future, it can be expected that machine and facilities containing information equipment will come into extensive use in medicine, education, pollution control, traffic control and all industrial areas. As this process continues, various kinds of robot-operated and control machinery and equipment will certainly be created.

The Development of Systems Industries

The third stage will be *the development of systems industries.* Analyses of the industrial structure have, in the past, generally been based on a quantitative assessment setting out the ratio of constituent industries, and the shift from low to high technology industries.

But the structure of the systems industries will consist of a complex of industries formed by linking up existing industries with the information industries. This means a qualitative change in the industrial structure, one example of which is seen in automatic warehousing, which has combined warehousing with the information industries. The systems industries may range from the relatively simple, such as automatic warehousing and automatic diagnosis systems to highly complex systems industries, such as the health industry and the opportunity industry.

The 'health industry' will comprise a system that includes food, pharmaceuticals, medical services, sports, and information, combined organically. The medical care industry of the future will not mean simply the treatment of disease. The emphasis will be on early diagnosis and the maintenance of health. Medical care, through the integration of new systems and technology, such as frozen food technology, preventive medicine, hospital automation, health diagnosis centers, and athletic clubs, can be expected to develop into a health industry that operates as a systems industry.

Table 9.1 Matrix Industrial Structure

by products	by systems	Distribution Industry	Integrated Transport Industry	Housing Industry	Regional Development Industry	Environment Industry	Marine Industry	Space Industry	Leisure Industry	Fashion Industry	Health Industry	Opportunity Development Industry
PRIMARY INDUSTRIES — Agricultural Industries	Mechanized Agriculture										●	
	Broiler Industry										●	
Fisheries Industries	Fish Hatcheries										●	
Mining Industries	Offshore Oil Wells						●					
	Underwater Mining						●					
SECONDARY INDUSTRIES — Light Industries	Manufactured Foods (Margarine, etc.)						●	●				
	Frozen Foods							●			●	
	Clothing									●	●	
	Cosmetics								●	●		
Heavy, Chemical Industries	Medical Supplies							●			●	
	Artificial Organs										●	
	Medical Engineering Equipment										●	
	Anti Air-Pollution Devices					●					●	
	Construction Equipment			●	●	●						
	Ambulances				●						●	
	Disaster Prevention Devices				●						●	
	Rack Style Warehouses		●		●							
	Deep Sea Submarines						●					
	Space Devices							●				
	Communications Satellites					●		●				
	Traffic Signal Equipment							●				
	Automated Commuter Transport		●		●				●			
Construction Industries	Prefabricated Houses			●	●							
	Mobile Homes			●					●			
	Hospitals			●	●						●	
	Highways		●			●			●		●	
	Land Development				●	●			●			

TERTIARY INDUSTRIES	Utility (Light, heat and power)	Atomic Power
		Solar Energy
		Natural Gas
	Traditional public Utilities	Regional Heating and Airconditioning Facilities
	Freight Industries	Monorail
		Container Transport
	Communications	Data Communications
	Commerce	Supermarkets
		Distribution Centers
	Warehousing	Warehouses
	Finance and Insurance	Opportunity Loans
		Housing Loans
	Personal Services	Medical Care
		Human Docks
		Athletic Clubs
QUATERNARY INDUSTRIES	Information Industries	Data Banks
		Computer Centers
		Software
		Computers
		Terminal Equipment
	Knowledge Industries	Think Tank
		Consultants
		Audiovisual Teaching Equipment
		CAI Equipment
		Color Television
	Arts Industries	Movies
		Plays
		Records
	Ethics Industries	Spiritual Training Centers
		Religious Groups
		Volunteer Service Groups

What we have called the 'opportunity industry' will be an integrated industry whose functions will be to open up personal possibilities for the future, and like the health industry, will be one of the systems industries that offers the possibility of personal growth.

The four major opportunity industries will be education, information, ethics, and finance-insurance, each with its own function. The education industries will promote the development of individual abilities. The information industries will supply information that will enable new opportunities to be discovered and created. The ethics industries will provide behavioral standards and guide in the molding of character, and the finance-insurance industries will provide needed capital and risk cover. The education industries will not operate on the current uniform system of school education, but will become a more diverse and dynamic system of education. Home self-learning, labor re-education, and computer plazas (where people can use the computer freely) will make their appearance. A mechanical data bank of enormous range will be established as an information industry, and the accumulation of information will proceed on everything necessary for opportunity development, from analysis of individual potential and work references to the location of educational facilities.

Training facilities for the ethics industries will be provided, and community centers where values and behavioral standards, thought, religion, and ethics are the focus of interest. The finance-insurance industries will be equipped to provide opportunity loans, the capital needed for the application of ability and opportunity development, and opportunity insurance as a guarantee against the risk of the loans.

The labeling of such systems industries should not be according to industrial categories used for traditional types of goods; the systems should be related to traditional categories of industries by means of a matrix. If the traditional categories of industry from primary to quaternary are placed on a horizontal axis, and systems industries are placed on the vertical axis, the relationship can be established. Table 9.1 sets out this new industrial matrix.

The primary industries divided into agriculture and forestry, stock-farming, fishery, mining, and manufacturing industries, are placed on the top portion of this industrial matrix. The more specific industries in each of these, such as mechanized agriculture and the broiler industry, are included. The industries shown in the matrix are those that bear some relation to the systems industries, which are on the horizontal axis. This matrix enables a multifaceted quantitative and qualitative analysis of the industrial structure to be made in a way that has not been possible before.

B. Expansion of the Public Economy

The second change in the economic structure will be *an expansion of the public economy.* Expansion of the public economy refers to an increase in the public side of economic activities, with the emphasis on economic activity for the public benefit rather than on profits to be made.

This expansion of the public economy will occur in four ways.

Strengthening of the Infrastructure

The first form of expansion will be *the strengthening of the infrastructure.* In the current industrial society, gas, water, communications, roads, parks, schools, etc., are typical examples of the infrastructure. But in the information society many other kinds of facilities and services will become important parts of the infrastructure. The most significant, needless to say, will be the information utilities.

In the information society, information utilities will be the driving force of social development. The information utilities themselves will basically assume the nature of an infrastructure, which alone will become a decisive factor in the transformation of the economic structure from the present private economy into a public economy in the information society.

In addition, *lands may also become part of the infrastructure* because these are limited basic resources that will take on the character of public assets, which will result from the separation of land ownership from use.

Of special note as infrastructure will be *do-it-yourself facilities.* These will be public facilities where many things can be done: carpentry, woodworking, ceramics, fabric dying, weaving, and even machine construction. These facilities will satisfy the need that people have to make things for themselves. Such places will be equipped not only with tools for handicrafts, but with highly sophisticated machinery and the needed technology; big facilities where people can make things for themselves that may take several months to complete. Hobbies for leisure-time activities are becoming more and more popular even now, but the information society will greatly increase free time, leading to increased desires to make things for oneself; so it is expected that these do-it-yourself facilities will develop to an astonishing degree, in sharp contrast with the antihuman automation-based production in present-day industrial society.

Basic Material Industies Join the Public Economy

The second form of expansion will be that *basic material industries join the public enterprises.* In the future information society, steel, oil refining, petrochemicals, fertilizers, synthetic fibers, aluminum, and other basic materials industries will probably all come into the public sector, for which there are two impelling reasons.

First will be the growing threat of shortages in basic material supplies, due partly to the depletion of natural resources, changes in climate, increases in population, and other factors. No matter how sophisticated technology becomes, it will not be possible for technology to produce adequate supplies of resources artificially, or for resources recycling to be total. Shortages in the supply of basic resources will inevitably become a major socio-economic factor, restricting the free economic activity of the private enterprise system.

A second reason why basic industries will become public is that in these basic materials industries automation by the use of computer technology will make very rapid progress. Already automation in industrial production has reached a fairly advanced stage, and before the beginning of the 21st century there will probably be massive and complete automation in basic industries, where the merits of scale are great, such as in the steel, petroleum, petrochemicals, cement and electric power industries. The increasing shortages in the supply of resources, conbined with the further expansion of productive power by applied automation will result in increased contradictions between the profit principle of monopolistic private capital and the public interest.

Expansion of Social Consumption

The third change in the public economy will be *the expansion of social consumption.* The dominant form of consumption in industrial society at present is individual, as evidenced by food, housing, automobiles, etc., all of which are commodities of personal consumption. The examples of social consumption are parks, roads, schools, hospitals, etc., but individual consumption carries far greater weight than social consumption.

In the information society, however, social consumption will constitute a far larger portion of total consumption than individual consumption, influenced by two factors. *The first* will be that individual consumption will reach saturation point, with increased social disutility. In developed countries, the share of individual consumption is rapidly decreasing. And social disutility, which includes air pollution, urban congestion, and the destruction of nature, is increasing in inverse proportion to the increase in material consumption. As these conditions increase, people will attach more importance to social utility, thus imposing restraints on individual consumption and enhancing the tendency for an increase in social consumption.

The second factor to encourage social consumption is that the basic characteristic of computer information is as a service offered by a public utility. In the information society this computer information will be used extensively by people in general through the information utility. There will also be a large number of social information network systems, such as the medical care information system and the education information system that will be essential to the maintenance of health and the development of capabilities.

C. The Shift to a Synergetic Economic System

We now consider *the shift from a free economic system to a synergetic economic system* in the information society, the total transformation of the economic system itself. This will be the final form, comprehensively encompassing the transformation of the economic structure so far outlined.

For the most part, the current economic system in industrial society has tended to be a liberalistic economic system characterized by (1) free competition of private enterprise, (2) pursuit of profits, (3) commodity production, (4) supply —demand as the determinant of prices.

But in the future information society, this liberalistic economy will be transformed into a new economic system, a synergetic economy, which is *an economic system based on synergism.* The three aspects of this are as follows:

Synergetic Production and Shared Utilization

First will be the transformation from a commodity economy to *a synergetic production and shared utilization economy.* Now the production of goods is at the core of economic activity, with production and consumption wholly separated. But future society will mean synergetic production and shared utilization, as constituting the primary economic system. The realization of this will be encouraged in two ways, one of which will be the development of information utilities. In the information society, information utilities will form the core of economic development. The unique production system of the information utilities will be structurally quite unlike factory production. As has been said, the production of information by the information utilities will differ structurally from the production of material goods by factories, in that it will be man-machine based production of information, characterized by self-multiplication. Information utilities will not merely provide extensive information processing and service to the general public. The information utilities will be used by the people themselves to produce the information they require. In addition, the programs produced by the people and the data they have collected will be available for shared utilization by all other persons. When this occurs, information utilities will advance to the synergetic production and shared utilization of information accumulated by the citizens. This unique production structure of the information utilities will not determine merely the production structure for information goods; it will broadly determine the structure of the consumption and distribution of information goods. Producers will also be users, and in this way the economic goods produced will be shared and utilized. And because the information utilities will be the axial institutions in the economy of the information society, the joint production and shared utilization of information goods will greatly influence the economic structure as a whole.

One more thing to be emphasized is that the people will voluntarily participate in the synergetic construction of public facilities. In the information society, it will become quite normal for the synergetic labor of citizens to construct public facilities such as homes for the elderly, parks, roads, and schools. Of course, national and local governments will provide part of the materials and funds, but the main characteristic of this kind of construction will be that the share of funds and physical and mental labor voluntarily contributed by the citizens themselves will be greater.

Voluntary Synergy to Achieve a Shared Economic Goal

The second aspect is that, corresponding to free competition, there will be voluntary synergy. This refers to individual economic subjects carrying on economic activities synergetically in order to achieve a shared economic goal.

In industrial society, private enterprises carry on business activites freely. The result has been that this free competition has meant the development of the national economy as a whole, and provided national economic welfare. This free competition in the micro enterprise economy has functioned effectively, without conflicting, on the whole, with the orderless macro national economy, because the law of price, Adam Smith's invisible hand, has guided and adjusted business activity. Behind Adam Smith's law of price, however, was the tacit economic assumption that resources are limitless, and if demand expands, the production of goods will go on expanding indefinitely.

But this economic assumption is now proving to be invalid; Smith's invisible hand is not functioning as effectively as in the past, because we have begun to recognize that resources are finite. The gigantic productive economic subjects have to give priority to carrying on economic activity to reach shared economic goals, which, in one sense, means voluntary synergy corresponding with free competition.

Autonous Restraints of Consumption

The third aspect is *the autonomous restraints of consumption by the people.* One economic principle of industrial society is the raising of consumption levels by mass production and mass consumption. But in the information society, autonomous restraints on the consumption of goods will apply to ensure stabilized development of the economy. The economic ethics of ordinary citizens will require that the limited natural resources must be used efficiently, and inflation prevented. The idea that the problems of shortages of natural resources and inflation will be resolved not by law imposed from above, but through voluntary restraints presents a new economic concept, worthy of the information society, and it is the concept and idea of the synergetic economy that lies at the base of this system.

Increased Management and Capital Participation

The fourth aspect will involve *an increase in management and capital participation.* The tendency for labor and the general public to participate in enterprises has already become a historical fact, and in the information society this tendency will certainly increase. The private side of private enterprise will decline, and the social side will increase as the public nature of economic activity expands from management participation to capital participation by labor and the general public. As this tendency progresses, there will be a change from authoritarian synergy to functional synergy in economic untis.

The synergetic relationships in economic groups in the existing economy are relationships of authoritarian synergy between the owner of capital, who has the right of management, and the employed workers. The lower strata has followed directions from above. But economic groups of the future will move toward an economic community of people who *participate voluntarily and share the same goal.* The synergetic relations that come into being will not be authoritarian but purely functional, which will probably come into being in stages by various methods and means; there will be management and capital participation by the general public, as well as *autonomous management.* What can be said clearly, is that the managerial class in the information society will not be a privileged class backed by monopoly ownership of capital and therefore the right of management; it will be *a functional class that has the job of management.*

This provides the general outline of the fundamental characteristics of the synergetic economic system. The synergetic economy will not suddenly replace the existing economy in the developing information society; rather, elements of the liberalistic economy will continue for a long time. For example, the pursuit of profits and the free prices and free markets of commodity production will not just suddenly disappear. What I am referring to is a gradual shift from the present economy to a synergetic economy in the sense that the hub of the economy in the information society will be a synergetic economic system, *with the trinity of contribution motive, voluntary synergy, and synergetic production with shared utilization.*

10
Participatory Democracy: Policy Decisions by Citizens

We want to take up the question now of a possible political system in the information society. If we may set out our conclusion first, we would say that the political system in the information society must be in the nature of *participatory democracy.* By this we mean a form of government in which policy decisions both for the state and for local self-government bodies will be made through the participation of ordinary citizens. The present political system is a parliamentary democracy in which the people elect representatives by vote, and the people participate only indirectly in decision making in the central government or local self-government entities, with political actions in the hands of the people's representatives. In other words, it acts as indirect democracy by means of indirect participation.

The Call for Participatory Democracy

The first reason why the political system in the information society will have to be changed from parliamentary democracy to participatory democracy, is that the *behavioral pattern of ordinary citizens will change.* They will be even less satisfied with mere material wants than they are now: *their chief desire will be for self-realization.* The satisfaction of material needs follows the process of production, distribution and consumption of material goods, while the quantitative and qualitative improvement of the people's material needs result from the increased capacity for material production and a better distribution of profits between capital and labor. In the long-range view, material production capacity grows at a much faster rate than the distribution in wages paid for labor.

An extreme example of this would be when material productivity of a given country grows 10-fold in half a century, whereas the absolute value of workers' earnings increases only five-fold, the distribution rate for labor standing at one half. The question we must ask is, what economic system can raise material productivity best to develop the economy? In industrial society, the liberal capitalist system has so far proved to be the most efficient socio-economic system. It was in this form that trade unions developed, to overcome the shortcomings of the system and prevent an inadequate distribution rate for labor, and raise the wage level.

The last phase of this process — consumption — means the physical consumption of material goods by individual persons, an entirely non-social act. What I want to stress here is that in industrial society, oriented toward the satisfaction of material needs, the liberal capitalist economic system has proved to be the most efficient social system; the public has given priority of this over other socio-economic and political systems, so long as material productivity grows to develop society and raise the level of material consumption. It can be said that because of this material satisfaction the demand of citizens for fuller participation in politics is reduced to a minimum.

However, in the information society, where the demand for self-fulfillment will become the motivation for action, the process of satisfying the people's demand for attaining objectives will find fulfillment in the production and utilization of information, the selection of action and the attainment of set aims. An economic system such as is most appropriate for promoting, expanding and improving our information productivity, and for promoting, expanding its use, will have to be a synergistic economic system based on synergetic production and joint utilization. This has already, been discussed in Chapter 9, 'A Synergistic Economic System.' The latter part of this process —selection of action and attainment of objectives— concerns the effects on the external environment of action taken by the doers, and is therefore closely related to the social and political fields.

This is the way in which, in the information society, people's desires will change direction toward the attainment of objectives, which will mean that their demand for participation in decision making and the management of the economic, social and political system will become stronger.

The second reason is that *the powers of the state and of commercial enterprises have greatly expanded,* and that *policy decisions made by such massive organizations cannot have far-reaching effects on the lives of ordinary people.* For instance, such issues as nuclear power generation, pollution, inflation—every one of these questions bears directly on the lives of ordinary people. Nevertheless, it is only by holding a national or local referendum that citizens can participate in policy decision on any of these vital issues.

The third reason is that *many of the questions that we have to decide are matters that concern all mankind, global issues that know no national boundaries, and the settlement of which directly affects the lives of all persons.* Take two examples: the question of the population explosion, and shortages of natural resources and energy; these diverse global issues override national borders, and while the activities of the United Nations and other international organizations through international cooperation will have an important role to play in resolving them. By far the more important role will be the voluntary cooperation of all citizens in resolving such global questions, and who can be expected to exercise restraints in their own lives. Take, for example, the question of the population explosion; this is a problem that can only be democratically resolved if throughout the world there are voluntary restraints accepted in the people's way of life, by which they restrict themselves to a basic replacement rate averaging about two children per couple. The only way to get cooperation in adopting such a principle is to secure the participation and agreement of citizens in working for such solutions.

The fourth reason is that *the technical difficulties, that until now have made it impossible for large numbers of citizens to participate in policy-making, have now been solved by the revolution in computer-communications technology.*

One of the major factors that have stood in the way of direct participation of ordinary citizens in national policy-making was technical. To consider any such proposition would have involved the work of a great number of personnel and a long period of time, and tremendous cost. This becomes clear if we recall how a national referendum is held.

But now the remarkable development of computer and communications technology has solved this problem at one stroke. The development of communication satellites in particular, and home computers, along with the time-sharing system, together offer a solution to the problems of personnel, time and costs. Furthermore, citizens would be enabled to participate not merely once but repeatedly, enabling them to understand more deeply, from many angles and in a long-range perspective, both the nature and the implications of the problems arising on any issue. From this cooperation would come the fairest, the most reasonable composite solution, so that a final solution from among all proposals will come from understanding and popular consent. We can add that the people would be enabled to participate from time to time in dynamically changing any solution adopted, taking into consideration the actual results of implementation of their selection, and consistent with changes in the objective situation.

Six Basic Principles

To enable this direct, participatory democracy of citizens to function effectively, it will be necessary to set the following six basic principles, which would have to be strictly and faithfully observed.

First principle: *All citizens would have to participate in decision making, or at least, the maximum number.*

All citizens interested directly or indirectly in any question proposed would have the right to participate in this system, irrespective of race, religion, age, sex, or occupation. It will be necessary to ease restrictions on the score of age, with the present voting age substantially lowered, to take in teenagers, depending on the questions to be decided. No democratic solution would be possible without the participation of the teen-age generation on such matters as smoking, education, sex, and others.

Second principle: *The spirit of synergy and mutual assistance should permeate the whole system.*

To ensure the smooth management of the system of participation, and so that it may be fully effective, the basic attitude of all participating in this system should be inspired by the spirit of synergy and mutual assistance. 'Synergy' means that *each person cooperates and acts from his or her own standpoint in solving common problems,* and 'mutual assistance' implies *readiness to voluntarily sacrifice one's own interests for the common good, to level out the disadvantages and sacrifices to other persons and/or groups.*

But synergism goes beyond cooperative effort. Synergistic cooperation brings a wider law into operation, in that the total effect of things acting together is greater than the sum of individual or separate effects achieved.

Parliamentary democracy as we now know it is a system by which the majority imposes its will and policies on the minority, according to the principle of majority rule. It is based on the spirit of individualism and egotism, a self-centered and aggressive attitude that needs to be radically changed to one that is altruistic and cooperative. This is not to be confused with mere collectivism, as it is wholly based on respect for each individual's freedom and interests.

Third principle: *All relevant information should be available to the public.*

When a question is to be resolved with the participation of all the citizens, all relevant information must be made public. In present industrial society, on questions most closely related to the living of the people, the major part of the relevant information is withheld on the grounds of national security or protection of enterprise secrets. But in the future information society, the principle of making information open to the public is a fundamental condition for citizen participatory democracy.

It is necessary that the public be informed not only on factual information, but also on all the possible social, economic and other effects on the lives of the people. Only in this way can each individual understand the problems in which he is interested, not one-sidedly or short-range, but with a broad, long-range perspective, and participate in the decision making not only from one's own standpoint but from the standpoint of the whole community.

In addition, *people will be expected to provide information voluntarily to contribute to a solution of any question.* In the information society, it will be rather this kind of information provided by citizens that will play the major role as basic data for the solution of various problems. Let us imagine that GIUs (global information utility systems) are formed and operated by world citizens. This would mean that information monitored at hundreds of thousands of points on the earth about meteorological conditions, air pollution, plant growth and other matters would be available daily to GIUs. There is no doubt that data so collected would prove to be a fundamental factor in helping mankind meet the changing meteorological and ecological conditions all over the earth.

Fourth principle: *All benefits received and sacrifices made by citizens should be distributed equitably among them.*

All problems that require participation for their solution are complex by their nature, and the way they are solved would affect different people differently, depending on their place in life and the circumstances in which they live. There would frequently be extreme cases in which those who are to benefit greatly from the solution of a certain problem will be sharply opposed by others who expect it not to profit them. People may also have different evaluations of a problem according to the value systems they cherish. Therefore, in solution of a problem that has a complex effect on the people, consideration must be given to the benefits received and sacrifices made as a result of its solution being distributed in a balanced way among such individual citizens and groups of citizens as are specifically interested in it in one way or another. The balance to be maintained in such cases would be by *combinations of the various benefits and sacrifices,* determined by *the nature and degree of effects* on individuals and groups in different places and positions, a balanced combination achieved with *a long-range perspective.* For instance, sacrifices would have to be balanced by compensations not only in terms of goods or monetary gains, but also, for example, in special educational opportunities for the children of those making the sacrifices; good offices that help in securing desired jobs or positions, or by some other non-economic means. In some cases, long-range political consideration will have to be given so that those who may have to make sacrifices without compensation in solving a certain problem may derive future benefit from the solution of other problems.

Fifth principle: *A solution should be sought by persuasion and agreement.*

A decision on the solution of a problem should, in principle, be made by the general agreement of all citizens concerned. Patient efforts will be needed to lead opposing individuals or groups to reach agreement. In our present parliamentary democracy, political deals and compromises are made in many cases between the ruling and opposition parties until a decision is reached on important policy matters, or action taken without agreement based on the principle of majority rule. But the information society will require that decisions be made by the *consent* of all participating citizens, and by *persuasion.* But to make this possible, the decisive point will be the above-mentioned conditions —the spirit of synergy, mutual assistance, publication of all relevant information and a balanced distribution of benefits and sacrifices. In case there are individuals or groups that, even after tireless persuasion, are still opposed to a proposed solution, a second solution put up by such individuals or groups would have to be adopted, out of respect for a minority view, the condition being, however, that such a solution does not impose hardship on other individuals or groups.

Sixth principle: *Once decided, all citizens would be expected to cooperate in applying the solution.*

The principle is that all citizens will be expected to cooperate in the implementation of a solution decided with their participation. This obligation is a corollary to the right to participate directly in policy-making, but it carries with it *the expectation of voluntary self-restraint,* and *should not assume the form of compulsion accompanied by punishment by enforcement of law,* as in the present industrial society. Participation in decision making, and the observance of the decision through voluntary self-restraints, are inseparable, and it is on this that a new policy-making system and a new social order will be based in the information society. Naturally, there will arise the problem of citizens who violate this social ethical code, but such violators would not be subject to punishment, but would be required to compensate by making *a social contribution*, or by rendering service to the community in some way to make amends for their failure to abide by the decision. The system would not be adjusted by punishment but by the reform of offenders.

Problems Concerning Participatory Democracy

Even if these six principle were to be observed, a number of basic questions would still have to be resolved for participatory democracy to function effectively.

The first question is *how to create and make available accurate and fair information.* More important than anything else for people to make proper policy decisions in a direct, participatory democracy is for accurate and fair information to be made available to them. If an organ to create and provide information were to be monopolized by a small group with a vested interest, and operated to serve that interest, or if specialists and engineers working for such an organ should process information according to their own specific values or ideology, citizens would be participating in policy-making on distorted or inaccurate information. To guard against this, the participation of the people in the management of such an organ responsible to create and provide information would be absolutely necessary.

The second problem is, *how will the people be able to participate in the settlement of problems that involve State sovereignty?* How can they participate in decisions on questions involving national defense or even war?

There have been recurring controversies over the question of policy-making on this kind of question between the military and a president or prime minister, or even between the Diet and the military. The main issue in such controversies is that of the need for instant action in the declaration of war, or in taking defensive measures in the face of enemy attack, or the disadvantage a country faces if a long time is required to make a decision on defensive military action.

But speaking from the basic concept of participatory democracy, it is precisely such important problems of the State that determine the future of a country, and in which all citizens are expected to participate. The only way to resolve this is for *the citizens to participate in peacetime,* in making decisions that will prevent a war from breaking out. As citizens come to participate in decisions on measures aimed at prevention of war, such as reduction of military spending and increased aid to developing countries, arguments calling for immediate military action will become increasingly untenable. But for these and other measures for the prevention of war to be really effective, citizens not only in one country, but also in countries that are in hostile relations with the former, will also be required to take concerted action, which stresses the need for international *or global citizen participation.*

The third problem is *how to deal with a problem that cannot be solved even by respect for a minority.* The most important aspect of policy-making by participatory democracy is that it aims at many-sided, complex solutions that take into account minority opinions, rather than seeking a single solution as in a parliamentary democracy. This method makes it possible to win the support of a majority of the citizens; but if a handful of citizens should stand out against a proposed solution, how far can the principle of respect for the minority be carried? There is only one way to settle this question. It is to carry out thorough *enlightenment and education such as will lead the citizens to adopt a spirit of synergy and mutual assistance;* the radical way of solving this is by directing such enlightenment and educational work not only at individuals or groups who may be opposed to such and such a solution, but also at all people from childhood in their homes and in schools, and in all their fields of activity.

Together with an objective-oriented pattern of behavior, this synergistic and mutual assistance spirit of the citizens is the most important for the information society.

11
Computer Privacy: Copernican Turn in Privacy

Approach to Computer Privacy from the Standpoint of Developmental Stages of Computerization

Human rights in relation to the computer revolution have been discussed mainly from the viewpoint of the invasion of privacy, but the following two points show that this kind of discussion does not meet the case. First, this issue is discussed in terms of the present problem of computer privacy, but the *long-term viewpoint is overlooked. The second* point is that this kind of discussion completely ignores the fact that the *information democracy will improve as information productivity increases.* This latter point is the decisive one.

The human right to information, that is, *the human right to know,* along with *the human right to protect secrets,* will be guaranteed by an increase in the production of information, and the human right to protect secrets is an issue involving the very right to privacy. In the information society, the human right to information will inevitably change both in nature and content in the course of the computer revolution.

Viewed thus, let us discuss computer privacy in its relation to the development of the information society from a long-range standpoint, and at the same time examine how this issue can be dealt with, especially in connection with changes in values and social and economic systems, such as can be expected to occur in the course of the development of the information society.[19]

In making this approach, it is necessary to introduce the concept of four developmental stages of computerization: big science-based, management-based, society-based and individual-based, which are already described in Chapter 4 ('Future Image of Information Society').

No Problem in the First Stage

The issue of computer privacy does not arise in the first stage of computerization.

In this stage of big science-based computerization, detailed personal data will have been collected on scientists, specialist engineers, military men and civilian staff members engaged in national defense and space development projects. Such data covers a number of items: birth, personal history, character, specialities, achievements, behavior, etc. of the persons concerned.

Such personal data records are strictly guarded by the government or military agencies directly under its control, limiting the possibility of such data being stolen or abused by a third party. Information on such persons is directly related to the maintenance of state secrets, and therefore the prevention of privacy invasion is the responsibility of the State.

Further, the question of privacy closely related to *national interests existed even before the question of computer privacy arose,* and strictly speaking, was not of the kind that should be taken up especially as computer privacy. It can therefore be concluded that the question of 'computer privacy' does not arise at the stage of big science -based computerization.

Not So Serious in the Second Stage

It is in this second stage, management-based computerization, that computer privacy in the information society *arises as an important issue.*

At this stage, various kinds of personal information are recorded and accumulated in large quantities by computers in the course of computerization under management control by government agencies and private enterprises.

Computers at this stage are used extensively for the automatic processing of large quantities of simple clerical work, repeated on a routine basis. For instance, government agencies introduce computer systems widely and effectively for the quick processing of work, and for the reduction of personnel costs; this includes the collection of taxes and the handling of social security work; and in enterprises, for keeping records of bank deposits, collecting life insurance premiums, electricity charges, etc. Personal data files of this kind previously existed in the form of card indexing and other systems, but the personal data filing system by computers has a number of merits which the conventional card system lacked, such as (1) quick retrieval of specific personal data, (2) integration of personal information from a number of data files, and (3) convenience in copying and transferring such data files.

This opens up the possibility of computerized personal data files *being misused for purposes other than originally intended,* either by the owners of such files or by a third person. This is the main reason for the question of computer privacy being raised.

The characteristics of computer privacy in this stage of management-based computerization can be listed as follows:

- The purpose of personal data files calls for efficient management.
- Data on ordinary citizens are filed by the central government and local governments and by enterprises.
- The filing of such personal data is based on a legal agreement or contract.
- Data are filed according to pre-determined common items.
- Data filers are, in principle, the users of the data files, and the filers have exclusive use of such files, but those whose data are filed do not directly benefit from the data.

The issue of computer privacy in this stage takes the following three different forms:

- Government controls over ordinary citizens are strengthened, and the freedom of citizens is violated if the central and local governments use personal data for purposes other than originally intended.
- Ordinary citizens suffer psychological, social or economic damage if enterprises use managerial personal data and administrative personal data to their own advantage.
- The right of ordinary citizens to privacy is violated if those personal data are disclosed to a third party.

In this stage, computer privacy has *a quantitatively broad application affecting all citizens,* but, at the same time, *the effect is limited* to the range of personal data recorded. For example, if an enterprise uses the registered names of residents for addressing direct mail, the objections of ordinary citizens do not go beyond the psychological irritation of receiving a lot of direct mail, sometimes called 'junk mail.'

Computer privacy in this stage actually embodies the following two points:

- If a unified national system of code numbers for all citizens is adopted, the danger will be that the central government or a local government may integrate all kinds of personal administrative records, and utilize such records for the purpose of thought control, or for other political purposes.

– Even if the harm to ordinary citizens is relatively slight, there is the danger that more serious invasions of privacy will be possible if slight infringements are accepted without protest.

The following two measures are therefore proposed to protect computer privacy at this stage:

– The government should not adopt a unified national system of code numbers for all citizens without *an effective watch-dog organ being set up by the citizens.*

– The government, a local government or an enterprise *should not be permitted to utilize or allow a third person to utilize personal data files other than as originally intended.*

If such measures are strictly enforced, computer privacy in this stage can be fully safeguarded.

Decisive Effect in the Third Stage

As computerization enters its third stage, the stage of society-based computerization, the question of computer privacy changes in *both character and content.* This is because computers at this stage will be used not only in management control by Government and enterprises, but also in wide social fields. Computerization will spread into such broad areas as traffic control, pollution prevention, medical care and education, and it will be computer files on personal information relating to these social activities that will have *a direct bearing on computer privacy.*

The following changes in character and content in the issue of computer privacy will occur:

– Personal data files will be compiled for the improvement of the social welfare of ordinary citizens and for the advancement of public interests.

– The filers of personal data will be confined to the government, local governments and other public organs.

– Personal data will be filed on the basis of a legal obligation or on a contract basis.

– Personal data will be filed according to approved detailed

items concerning the private and social life of individuals.
- Data files will be utilized by both the data filers and those about whom data is filed.
- Those whose data is filed will be able to benefit from the files.

The issue of privacy will change in nature and contents as follows:

- If the State should misuse personal welfare data for purposes other than originally intended, government controls on particular persons or groups of persons would be strengthened and *a citizen's right to freedom seriously violated.*
- If an enterprise should utilize these personal files for management control, *particular persons or groups would suffer considerable psychological, social or economic harm.*
- If existing general administrative records or enterprise records should be combined with these welfare records, the scope of privacy invasion would be widened and its degree deepened.

Computer privacy in the stage of society-based computerization would be confined to particular persons or groups of persons, and in this respect, the scope of this problem would be narrowed down, but its effect would become incomparably greater than in the stage of management-based computerization. Thus, *particular personal data of one kind can have a decisive effect on the life of persons whose data is filed.* By way of example, detailed records on the history of an illness of a person could deprive that person of an opportunity for employment. Further, school records or behavioral records of a person from childhood could reveal character, ability, thought and social background, and could be a decisive factor in determining a future career, including employment, marriage, etc.

The following two measures would be necessary to safeguard computer privacy:

- File management and utilization of personal data on welfare matters should be *under the control of a committee consisting of representatives of public organs and citizens,* with the latter comprising an overwhelming majority of the committee.
- *A series of social and economic measures would be needed to prevent anyone from suffering social disadvantages* that could arise from personal data files on welfare.

Measures against privacy invasion in this stage could be taken a step further by provision of legal countermeasures, or by a citizens' watch-dog organization; it would also be necessary for *the represen-*

tatives of citizens to participate directly in the management of personal data files, with the citizens empowered to supervise the files. Further, various social and economic measures would be needed to prevent anyone suffering social disadvantages from the existence of the files. This is of special importance. In more concrete terms, it will be necessary to introduce *a system of social compensation* by which anyone suffering a social disadvantage may secure an opportunity of employment and a stable social life. It would be possible to resolve the problems of computer privacy in this stage by introducing such measures and creating a societal environment to adopt such measures.

Copernican Turn in the Fourth Stage

In this stage, the information utilities will play a leading role in the information society. By 'information utility' we mean a public information infrastructure available to everyone at low cost, at any time or place. Each individual citizen will be able to obtain the needed information, solve problems and seek future possibilities by the creation of highly sophisticated information, merely by connecting the home terminal to the information utility. It is in such a society that all citizens will be able to experience the full blooming of the flower of life. In this stage of high mass knowledge creation, computer privacy will *change in character and content* as set out below:

- Personal data files will be used by people to solve the problems of individuals and for the development of their own opportunities.
- The filers will belong to the public infrastructure.
- The filing of personal data will be by voluntary registration.
- Personal data files will cover all items relevant to the private and social life of individuals.
- Users of personal data files will be restricted to those whose data is filed.

In this case, the preservation of computer privacy will become more serious in character and content in the following ways:

- If the Government should misuse personal data for administrative or political purposes other than originally intended, *all citizens could be completely regimented and deprived of their freedoms.*
- If an enterpise should utilize such personal data files for the purpose of management control or its own advantage, *all citizens*

would suffer decisive psychological, social or economic and political damage.

In this way, if such personal data files should be misused especially by groups in positions of power, the information society would be turned into a fearful regimented society, and the right of citizens to freedom and protection against privacy invasion would come under a completely polarized, antinomistic relationship.

But if personal data files are utilized for the benefit of the persons concerned, they will *bring inestimable benefits* to them, whereas if abused by other persons or organizations, the files would become a *means of completely controlling the people's destinies.*

The following essential preconditions will be necessary to prevent computer privacy invasion taking place in this stage:

- Information utilities should be *completely controlled and managed autonomously by citizens.*
- *New political, economic and social systems should be introduced* to make it possible for such autonomous controls on personal data files to be exercised by the people.

This latter pre-condition is especially necessary. By new systems we mean such new political systems as will be established in concrete terms by a transition from the present parliamentary democracy of indirect participation to *a democracy of direct participation,* and a new economic system through the transition from our present so-called liberal economic system centering on private enterprises to *a synergetic economy,* in which the infrastructure will play a leading role. Such a new social system will be realized through a transition from the present system which centers on material consumption, to a life-style centered on *the creation of knowledge.* In short, the future information society will need to be a citizens' society of a new type, a participatory, synergetic and knowledge-creating society.

Put another way, it will be within the framework of a citizens' society of this new type that information utilities will be autonomously controlled by citizens, and all individual citizens will be free to let their creativity express itself. And if the information society is transformed into a citizens' society of this new type, computer privacy will of necessity undergo a basic change, because, in a synergetic society of knowledge-creation and under conditions of complete, autonomous control of information utilities by the citizens, it will be to the advantage of all citizens to make their own personal data files available in the information utilities as openly as possible, and for all to utilize each other's personal files jointly. This will ultimately make a great contribution to the citizens' society as a whole.

In other words, records on the solution of problems and opportunity developments of individual citizens, and the data gathered for this purpose, will be of great value to other people as well for problem solving, and for opportunities development. Not only that, these data will be important for the solution of problems that are common to all citizens.

Computer privacy will thus undergo a radical qualitative change. The issue of privacy, which arose as a fundamental human right in the course of the development of modern civilized society, will *lose most of its historical significance.*

Even the human right to information will change drastically in character. *The human right to know will change into a human right to utilize information and the human right to protect secrets will change into a human duty or ethic to share information.* This can be described precisely as a Copernican turn in personal privacy.

Conclusion

Computer privacy changes greatly in nature and content according to the stages of development of information society. Table 12.1 sets out these changes in computer privacy, and the following four important tendencies can be read from this table:

1. There is a tendency for the purpose of personal data files to *change gradually from national and enterprise interests to social interests;* and in keeping with this, the beneficiaries of data files will also change from the State, the military and local governments to local communities and individuals.
2. The scope of privacy invasion tends to widen from a limited number of persons or groups to ordinary citizens, and *the degree of privacy invasion to increase from a minimum to a maximum.*
3. Further, measures against privacy invasion tend to develop *from legal restraints* on the utilization of personal data files *to citizens' participation in and autonomous control of information administration organs,* and *to the transformation of societal systems and institutions.* That is, from technical measures to the form of control and transformation of social institutions.
4. In the course of these changes, the nature of the issue of privacy itself gradually changes, and the possibility is that ultimately *it will lose its historical significance.*

Table 11.1 Changes in Computer Privacy, Viewed from the Standpoint of Developmental Stages of Computerization

	1st Stage Big science-based	2nd Stage Manage-ment-based	3rd Stage Society-based	4th Stage Private person-based
Forms of personal data files	National security files	Management data files	Social data files	Personal data files
Purposes of files	Maintenance of State secrets	Efficient management control	Increased social welfare	Development of individual opportunities
Filers	Government, the military	Government, local govern-ment, enter-prises	Government, local govern-ments, public organs	Public organs
Those whose data are filed	Limited number of specific persons	Ordinary citizens	Ordinary citizens, local residents	Local residents
File items	Detailed information on individ-uals	Formulated common items	Formulated common items, and special items	Non-formu-lated special items
Benefici-aries of files	Filers	Filers	Filers and those whose data are filed	Those whose data are filed
Privacy invasion Scope	small (limited number of persons)	Great ordinary citizens)	Medium (specific persons, groups)	Great (ordinary citizens)
Degree	Infinitesimal (hardly any privacy invasion)	Small (psycholo-gical)	Medium (social, economic damage)	Extremely great (regi-mented society)
Measures against privacy invasion	Direct control by Govern-ment, military	Legal restraint Technical measures Watch-dog organs	Joint commit-tee of filers, those whose data are filed Social measures aimed at re-ducing the disadvantages of those whose data are filed	Autonomous control by those whose data are filed Transforma-tion of societal systems aimed at eliminating violations of the privacy of those whose data are filed

12
Information Gap: Simultaneous Solution of a Dual Gap

Information Gap as a Dual Gap

Along with the problem of the invasion of privacy by computers, which is certain to be faced in the move toward the information society, there is a problem of the information gap. This information gap exists as an information technology gap between industrialized and developing countries, a gap more serious than the present industrial gap that separates them. The industrial gap is one of productive technology, the main obstacle to its solution being the lack of financial resources in developing countries; but the information gap means the relative absence of information processing and transmission technology, to which must be added the human factors of levels of intellectual development and behavioral patterns in such countries. These, more than the lack of financial resources, are a major obstacle to technological transfers.

The problem is all the more serious because *the information gap overlaps the industrial gap,* together forming a double gap. If this dual technological gap continues to exist between industrial and developing countries, serious anarchical antagonisms will come in to plague human society. [20]

First, there will be *increased cultural discontinuity between them.* We are aware of the serious gap between the peoples of under-developed countries, and the peoples of industrialized countries, but amongst such peoples of under-developed countries there is already positive curiosity and interest in the products of the advanced countries, and such people can now board a plane to visit the industrial world if they have funds. But the societal gap of the future between industrialized countries and developing countries could be incomparably more serious, and mean even complete cultural discontinuity, because the gap is one in intellectual communication essential for mutual understanding.

The second confrontation would be due to *the exhaustion of natural resources,* plus *the environmental disruption* and *the population explosion.* Many developing countries have set out to reach their national goals of industrialization, modernization and improved living standards.

But if developing countries push ahead with industrialization by following the same course followed by the industrialized countries in the past, it will be all the more difficult to resolve current problems, already becoming very serious, such as the exhaustion of natural resources, the destruction of natural surroundings and the population explosion, which could precipitate humanity into a catastrophic crisis.

In the autumn of 1978, some U.S. scholars engaged in research on nuclear fusion held free discussions on the question: 'What will become of human society if nuclear fusion is developed as a practical technical achievement, and if, in the coming and following centuries, energy can be supplied sufficiently using as material the inexhaustible heavy hydrogen in sea water?' The conclusion reached was as follows:

> If humankind is foolish enough to use energy so freely, on the grounds that there is no longer need to worry about it, and if the consumption of energy is increased by 10 percent annually, the total amount of energy consumed on the earth will amount over 100 years to the same as the sun's energy received on the surface of the earth. This would render the planet no longer habitable. (Yomiuri Shimbun, Aug. 17, 1979)

Third, the development of the information society in industrialized countries could be promoted in *an extremely distorted way, assuming a totally military and undemocratic nature.* The sharpening of contradictions between industrialized and developing countries could result in intensified antagonisms and conflicts over security, especially involving the availability of natural resources among industrialized countries, as well as between them and developing countries. The result would be that industrialized countries would tend to utilize their advanced information technology in the use of communication satellites fundamentally for military purposes.

Further, this technology could be used domestically to restrain and control the free private lives and social activities of citizens. Personal privacy could be freely invaded, and the people's autonomous social and political activities could be suppressed, to make the fearful, automated Orwellian state a reality.

Simultaneous Promotion of Industrialization and Informationalization

In order to combat this frightening prospect, it is essential to modify and ultimately eliminate the dual gap of industrialization and information, for which the best, in fact, the only alternative is the simultaneous promotion of industrialization and information technology in developing countries. Simultaneous promotion of information and industrial technology will *not cause any conflict* between these two kinds of technology, and given proper means and methods, it will not only greatly promote the industrialization of developing countries but will contribute toward *the creation of a new international order,* involving advanced countries.

By proper means and methods, I mean the following:

1. It is necessary to establish a system of government-led international technical assistance.
2. In introducing industrial technology, the emphasis should be placed on (1) *pollution-free,* (2) *resources conservation* and (3) *intellectual labor-saving industrial technologies.*
3. In introducing information technology, special attention will have to be paid to (1) *the construction of the information infrastructures* (2) *the introduction of social information systems,* including medical and educational systems.

In regard to item 1, it must be emphasized that no attempt should be made to transplant a uniform system in developing countries, but that *various different forms of technical aid* should be provided, consistent with the wide diversity of the countries concerned.

There is great diversity in developing countries, but they are capable of being classified into two major groups; (1) those countries that have already completed the initial stage of industrialization and could be called half developed countries and (2) those that are still to begin industrialization. The latter group can be subdivided into (1) countries rich in natural resources and (2) poor countries that depend mostly on agriculture and livestock raising.

It is necessary to take all such conditions into consideration rather than mechanically introducing new technology to them.

In the case of half-developed countries, it may be possible for them to follow *the policy of national capital cooperating with foreign capital,* and for countries rich in natural resources to pursue *the policy of state capital introducing advanced technology,* and for poor developing countries to *receive technological assistance from developed countries.*

In reference to item 2 (countries rich in natural resources) *labor saving* (engineers and managers) *industrial technologies* are extremely important to developing countries for the establishment of *a new system of international division of labor,* and also for the economic development of the countries concerned.

It is expected that in a new system of international division of labor, iron and steel and oil-refining industries will be developed mainly in countries where the raw materials exist. Importance will therefore be attached to assistance in *pollution-prevention technology* from an ecological standpoint. Further, the conservation of natural resources is a global responsibility to be shared both by industrialized countries and developing countries. In the introduction of intellectual labor-saving industrial technology, this is expected to have a dual effect, viz., solving the problem of shortages of engineers and managers without causing social distortions of unemployment, and promoting the development of the economies of developing countries. Industrial technology is inseparable from highly sophisticated information technology. In this sense, the induction of the former may be regarded as a form of information technology.

Item 3 (poor countries without natural resources), which deals with *the construction of the first information infrastructure,* shows that it is necessary to form a nationwide information and communication network. This should not consist merely of communication lines for telegrams and telephones, but should be *a digital communication network* permitting the use of computers for transmission and exhange of data. The reason is that we are now in *an era of electro-communication networks* for complex information media, including telephones, TVs, computers and fascimile systems. It is also necessary that such a communication network should form part of a global communication network, making use of communication satellites.

On the introduction of social information systems, it can be pointed out that in developing countries there are strong potential needs for the application of information technology to social areas, including regional development, medical care and education. But the need for information technology in enterprises is not so great, contrasting sharply with the strong need for such technology in advanced countries. There are hardly any large-scale, modern industrial enterprises in developing countries, so the management of information technology in developing countries will be oriented from the beginning toward *its utilization for social purposes.* Emphasis will be on the introduction of information technology to serve such areas as *medical care and education.*

Fig. 12.1 Industrial and Information Technology Policy Chart for Developing Countries

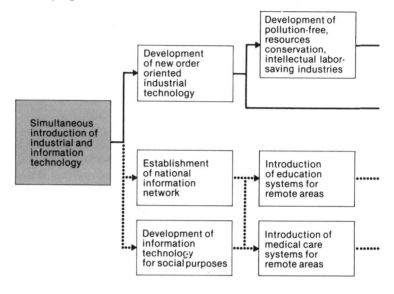

There are acute shortages of medical care and education staff and facilities in developing countries, and the large-scale introduction of medical care and education systems in remote areas, making full use of information technology, will greatly increase productivity by medical care and education. Problems which have been considered impossible to solve in the past—the elimination of illiteracy and the eradication of endemic diseases—can be solved for the first time in this way.

Integrated Results of Simultaneous Development of Industrial and Information Technology

If the simultaneous management of industrial and information technology is promoted in developing countries on the abovementioned principles, the following integrated results will be possible:[21] (See Fig. 12.1)

The first result will be the narrowing of the industrial and information technology gap. If developing countries succeed in introducing conservation of pollution-free resources and intellectual labor-saving industrial technology, along with information technology

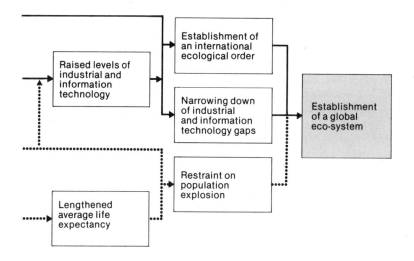

centering on education systems for remote areas, industrial and information technology will be able to be developed rapidly. The raised levels of education in particular will make it possible to train modern industrial workers and information engineers, and so lay the foundations for modern industry and for the future development of knowledge-intensive industries.

The second result will be preparation for an international ecological order. Since these countries will be oriented toward the development of pollution-free and material-saving industrial technology, such a development in these countries will surely contribute toward the establishment of an international ecological order.

The third result will be restraint on population explosion. The introduction of a medical care system for remote areas will temporarily have a negative effect, in that it will improve the health of the peoples in developing countries and lengthen their average life span. But on the other hand, the raised levels of education will increase the understanding among the people of the need for birth control and will make it possible to check the population explosion.

By this means, in the long run, it will be possible to *accomplish the common task of mankind—establish a global eco-system.*

Desirable and Feasible Approach

The approach to a global eco-system is not a mere dream. I mention three points to support the ideal. *The first* is, as the energy crisis makes clear, the compelling need in the world of today for a new world order and a new system of international cooperation. *The second* is that pollution-free, resources-saving industrial technology and information technology have been developed, and already many systems utilizing such technological developments are in practical operation. *The third* point is that information technology is both public and international in character, a point that must receive special emphasis. As has already been repeatedly stated, information is by nature public property; it is non-expendable, non-transferrable and has a cumulative effect. Fundamentally, information knows no national boundaries. As communication satellites whirl around the earth, conditions for the formation of a global information network already exist.

It is to be expected that industrialized countries will take the following steps as a desirable and realizable approach:

1. *To introduce resources-saving, energy-conserving and pollution-free industrialization,* such as will be acceptable to developing countries, and to formulate *a clear-cut action program* in line with this.
2. For industrialized countries *to reduce their armaments to at least one half in the 1980s,* and to use the funds thus saved to provide technical aid for developing countries.
3. For advanced countries of the world *to establish an international system of assistance in information technology* of a new type, which could bear the name of IIO *(International Information Organization).*

If industrialized countries and developing countries cooperate and keep in step as they move toward realization of these concepts, mankind not only will be able to avert many crises, such as the exhaustion of natural resources, the population explosion and the like, but the opportunity and perspective of a new global society full of entirely new possibilities will emerge.

13
The Goal Principle: New Fundamental Principle of Human Behavior

The Material Principle as Traditional

It is necessary that there be a fundamental principle of human behavior underlying the formation, maintenance and development of human society, which we may call *the societal principle.*

Unlike other animals, man has an innate desire not only for existence but for improvement and better living. Various means of subsistence have been created to satisfy these desires and improve living standards by utilizing these means. This process may be expressed as a process of satisfaction of human needs, as set out below:

> Human needs → production of means to satisfy human desires → satisfaction of human desires

This cyclical pattern of the satisfaction of human needs moves through a spiral, a qualitative development corresponding to the development of societal productive power.

When a development occurs in societal productive power, the boundaries of satisfaction of human needs expand; new needs arise with the development of the means to satisfy such needs. The basic pattern of the satisfaction of human needs may be plotted as follows:

Fig. 13.1 Basic Cyclical Pattern of Satisfaction of Human Needs

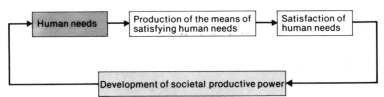

So that this cyclical pattern of the satisfaction of human needs may be maintained and developed in an orderly way, it is necessary for human beings as a whole to maintain social existence with some set of common values, and with a common consciousness of the need to realize these values.

This basic principle of human behavior is what we mean by the societal principle.

In the past, the human race went through three types of society— hunting, agricultural and industrial — and the boundaries of human needs have expanded according to the development of societal productive power. Nevertheless, the human race has continued to follow the material principle as the societal principle on which the formation, maintenance and development of human society has depended.

The reason is that human society has maintained a common societal principle bearing the following three features:

1. Human needs have been oriented toward the satisfaction of material needs.
2. The societal productive power, which is basic to the satisfaction of human needs, has been material productive power.
3. The satisfaction of human needs has been achieved mainly through the production and consumption of material things.

Thus, the development of hunting techniques, forming the base of the evolution of hunting society, represented advances in man's capacity to capture animals; which means an increase in material productive power in that it served to increase supplies of food and clothing for each person, and by this improvement in material productive power enabled the urgent needs of life to be met, the need to protect the members of the tribe from hunger and cold.

Then, agricultural productive power, which was the base on which agricultural society was built, represented advances in the capacity to produce material goods in the form of agricultural produce, by which mankind was able to secure food more than enough to sustain life. In these ways, human needs expanded their boundaries from the satisfaction of hunger to the satisfaction of the need for clothing, shelter, and the means of everyday living. Still human needs were oriented to the production of material goods.

In industrial society, the enormous development of industrial productive power made it possible to mass-produce goods, greatly extending the boundaries of mankind's material needs, and making it possible for all to enjoy a life of abundance as consumers, rightly called the flowering of material civilization.

Emergence of the Goal Principle

But in the information society, a wholly different societal principle makes its appearance; viz., the goal principle. This goal principle will have the following main characteristics:

1. Human needs will be oriented toward pursuit of *a self-determined goal.*
2. Societal productive power, which will be the basis for the satisfaction of human needs, will be *information productive power.*
3. Human needs will be satisfied through *the process of production of information and goal-oriented action.*

The traditional material principle and the goal principle may be compared, with respect to their basic cyclical pattern in the satisfaction of human needs, as follows:

Fig. 13.2 Comparison of the Material Consumption Type and Goal-achievement Type Cyclical Pattern of Satisfaction of Human Needs

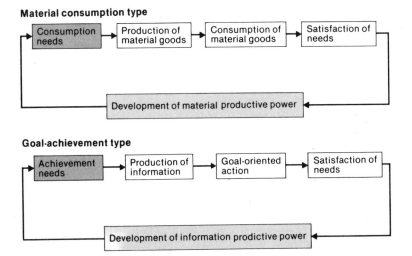

This change-over of the societal principle from the material to the goal-oriented principle will be brought about by *a change from material values to human values,* resulting in part from the shortfall in natural resources, increased pollution, and environmental disruption, helped by the remarkable expansion of knowledge-creating-information productive capacity, and due in the main to the development of computer-communications technology. We need to note that the goal principle differs fundamentally from the material principle in the satisfaction of needs. There is a change from the pattern of production and consumption of material goods to the production of information, leading to goal oriented action.

An examination of this basic change in the process of satisfaction of human wants will reveal the structural characteristics of the goal principle.

The structural characteristics of the goal principle may be examined from two angles, *the logic of situational reform and synergistic feedforward.*

The Logic of Situational Reform

What does 'situational reform' mean? We mean the replacement of the two processes; the process of production and consumption of material goods, and the process of production of information and goal-oriented action by situational reform, or the processes of value-realization on the same dimension.

Here 'situational reform' means *a process in which the current situation is changed into a new situation that is consistent with the subject's goal,* as expressed by the following formula:

Situation A   → Situation A'   → Realization of a value
(Current   (Desirable   (Satisfaction
situation)   situation)   of a want)

Let us apply this 'logic of situational reform' to the process of production and consumption of material goods.

First, the universal concept of economic production is of man making goods that satisfy human wants. That is to say, by the use of physical ability allied to tools and machines, etc., natural resources and raw materials are converted to goods for use. We can define the process of goods production as *the process by which natural resources are converted by goal-oriented action into goods that are useful.*

Let us take the example of hand-made bows and arrows. These are made by converting bamboo etc. and birds' feathers into bows and arrows. By the same principle, consumer durables like television sets are produced. In the case of television sets, natural resources such as iron, copper, and oil are first transformed into materials by application of the laws of physics and chemistry, which are then made into the many components, and finally these parts are assembled to provide something for use. This reveals a great difference in complexity for goal-oriented labor for the production of goods; but the basis of production is *the change of natural resources into a state in which all goals coincide*, a process which is the same for television as it is for bows and arrows.

What process of situational reform does reaching one's goal-oriented action represent? For example, suppose one sets the goal of 'owning a house to live in' and then goes on to achieve this goal. It will mean a change from the specific situation of living in an apartment to the new situation of living in a house of one's own. From the point of view of goods produced, this is a change into the form of durable goods, i.e., a house. From the point of view of goal-oriented action it can be defined as a goal-conforming change in one's living situation from a rented apartment to house ownership.

Let us take another example. If I set the goal of becoming a department manager in the company where I work, and then attain it, it is a goal-conforming change from one situation to another. Assuming that until then I had been a section chief, to move from the post of section chief to department manager is simply a change in my employment status in the company.

Seen in this way, production-oriented action, (economic action for the goal of material production) and goal-oriented actions, are exactly the same, in that they are a change from one situation to another, brought about by a subject.

The development, therefore, from the process of production→consumption of material goods to the process of information production →goal-attaining action, may be conceived of as a qualitative development of the *logic of situational reform*. Viewed from this standpoint, *both the material principle and the goal principle can be unified as the situational reform principle*, and the material principle may be encompassed by the goal principle in the broad sense of the word, in as much as the material principle is objective-oriented action for the satisfaction of material needs. The goal principle as used here, is therefore, in the narrow meaning of the term, restricted to the satisfaction of goal achievement needs, which are on a plane of higher human desire.

Need for New Interdisciplinary Social Sciences

If this concept of production is adopted, the production of material goods forms only one part of the concept, and broader, objective-oriented acts have to be included.

If a person undertakes an objective-oriented act, a start will be made by gathering the information necessary for the attainment of the set goal or by producing such information for oneself.

Next is the goal-oriented action necessary to purchase and produce goods and tools needed in reaching the goal. Sometimes the goal-oriented action may be sold in the form of labor, the immediate goal being to acquire funds needed to buy the essential goods and tools, and when necessary, part of the goal-oriented action must be used to persuade other people who have something to do with the same field to cooperate in the action. In extreme cases, changes will be necessary in laws, systems, and customs, in which case goal-oriented action will have to be given to win the cooperation and support of governments, politicians, and citizen groups. Such types of goal-oriented action will necessarily be deeply involved not only in economics but in politics and society as a whole.

When fellow citizens are persuaded to take part in action or to cooperate, the goal-oriented action carried on with others becomes a social action, and the goal-oriented action used to change laws or the policies of national and local governments in the direction desired is fundamentally political action. This concept means that the existing system of sciences, each operating in its own closed domain, will not be adequate as a system of science to meet the needs of the information society in which the principle of a set goal to be attained must operate as the primary principle of action. It will be necessary to establish a new system of interdisciplinary social sciences, in which sociology and behavioral sciences and not economics will hold the predominant place.

Let me emphasize the relevance to today of Max Weber's system of sociology, which set out its basic method as follows:

> We can examine social action, which may appear to be subjective, by objectively examining and regarding motives as being a cause-and-effect relationship.[22]

Weber uses the example of a crowd walking. They may appear to be simply walking, but actually they are going to a horse race. The action of walking may appear to be subjective but is actually objective.

In other words, he considered that human behavior is motivated and objective-oriented, and it is possible to trace objective cause-effect relationships in the social process if the relationship of means and objective is translated into a cause and effect relationship.

If social action is not impulsive or irrational but is objective-oriented and rational, it is possible to *replace the term objective-means oriented action with the term cause-effect relation,* as Weber says, and as has been said already. The goal principle will be firmly established as the first principle of human behavior in the information society. Then the social actions of citizens in general will become goal-means relationships that can be regarded as cause-effect relationships.

Four Types of Feedforward System

As for synergistic feedforward, we must begin by examining the relevance of the logic of situational reform to the feedforward system. As already explained, 'situational reform' means a change from the existing situation to a more desirable one, a process in which the subject of action works on the external environment to make it more desirable; this may be expressed as *a feedforward from the current situation to a desirable situation*. By 'feedforward' is meant *control in moving toward a goal*, and viewed from the standpoint of the subject of action, it means *a controlled development of the current situation to change it to a more desirable situation*. And included in this process of feedforward is not only the external environment on which the subject of action works, but also the subject of action itself.

The action for situational reform, viewed from this standpoint, is precisely the process by which the subject of action controls itself to adapt to a desirable situation. In this sense, situational reform is *a simultaneous feedforward process* by the subject of action and its external environment for realizing a desirable situation.

There are various feedforward systems as processes of situational reform. We may classify these into the following four types: (See Fig. 13.3)

1. Dependent feedforward
2. Controlled feedforward
3. Balanced feedforward
4. Synergistic feedforward

By 'dependent feedforward' we mean *one by which the subject of action exercises control in attaining the objective*, especially when the subject of action is dependent greatly on the external environment. This feedforward process is a negative and passive one.

The 'controlled feedforward' means that *the subject of action is in control of the external environment in a mutual relationship of forces*, a process in which the subject of action exercises control to bring the external environment into line with what is desired. This process is active and positive and takes the character of external control.

In 'balanced feedforward' *the subject of action and the external environment exercise mutual control if their relations are in balance.* This could mean mutual control of a competitive or antagonistic nature.

The 'synergistic feedforward' means that *the subject of action and the external environment are in mutually complementary relations and act together to reach a common objective.* This is a synergistic, mutually complementing, and integrated process of control.

In human society, however, the feedforward system assumes a far more complicated form, because it involves a feedforward system between the human and the natural environment, as well as between person and person within human society. These are not independent of each other; their relationship is such that the former is primary and the latter secondary and subordinate. In other words, at the stage of human development in which a certain kind of feedforward system between mankind and nature begins to function, a corresponding feedforward system between person and person within human society arises. This is because the development of human society requires a feedforward process between humans and nature that is favorable to humans; and further, in this development of human society, the process of social stratification of human society proceeds gradually.

Tracing the historical development of feedforward systems in human society, one finds an interesting phenomenon; that in human society, the feedforward system began as a dependent one, which is due now to be replaced by a higher synergistic one.

Dependent Feedforward and Taboos

The feedforward system, operating as a situational reform process, functioned in primitive society in the form of taboos. To primitive man. the natural environment was chaotic for a very long period of time, but gradually nature and the universe came to be regarded as ruled by a powerful god. From this, the idea that man should obey this god and adapt his own life to a natural order became prevalent in society, and with this came taboos as the first form of feedforward system. Taboos molded a social order that conformed to the natural order, and in effect were a dependent feedforward principle based on religious norms.

Taboos formed a system of passive dependent feedforward among human beings, on *the concept of divine laws,* leaving no room for voluntary action selection by human beings.

Fig. 13.3 Four Types of Feedforward Systems

1st type	Dependent feedforward system	Subject of action	←	External environment	The subject of action is dependent on the external environment in the feedforward process.
2nd type	Controlled feedforward system	Subject of action	→	External environment	The subject of action controls the external environment in the feedforward process.
3rd type	Balanced feedforward system	Subject of action	→ ←	External environment	The relations of forces between the subject of action and the external environment are balanced for mutual control in the feedforward process.
4th type	Synergistic feedforward system	Subject of action	⇒	External environment	The subject of action and the external environment cooperate to reach a common objective in the feedforward process.

Controlled Feedforward and Ruling Power

In agricultural society a new type of feedforward system operated. This was controlled feedforward in *the form of absolute rule* by one class over another, usually that of a feudal lord over peasants.

Here we see the operation of a feedforward system within human society, the background of which is a partial change of the feedforward system between man and the natural environment from a dependent system to a controlled system. Even in agricultural society, the universe was conceived of as ruled by the will of a god or gods, and the divine rules largely determined human behavior. So, the dependent feedforward system was deeply rooted in human society in the relations between mankind and the natural environment. However, mankind developed agricultural techniques and succeeded in turning vast expanses of wild land into arable land.

Only the feudal lord and a small class of knights took goal-oriented social action. All the peasants could do was follow these actions and yield to the power of their rulers; they could take no other social action. They were bound to the land and not permitted to leave it. Heredity determined one's occupation. And it was the peasant's mandatory duty to deliver tribute to the lord in the form of a part of the harvest produced each year. The rule of the feudal lord functioned as a single and absolute controlled feedforward law that encompassed all political, economic, and social aspects of living.

Balanced Feedforward and Price Mechanism

After this historical development, balanced feedforward came into being as a new feedforward system in industrial society. This came into being on *market principles and the price mechanisms* that automatically brought some kind of economic order into industrial society, such as, in Adam Smith's terms, the commercial transactions guided by self-interest in the give and take relations of *homo economus*, and the changes in market prices brought about by that *invisible hand*. At the micro level, there has certainly been balanced feedforward in the sense that the seller and the buyer have maintained economic order by each exercising self-control in economic operations, while bargaining in the market place. And at the macro level there has been balanced feedforward of the macro economy, consisting of the accumulation of balanced micro level feedforward (in the sense that a large number of enterprises are guided by the invisible hand of changes in market prices): supply and demand have balanced, and, in general, order has prevailed in the overall economy.

Behind this balanced feedforward in industrial society there has been controlled feedforward involving nature, *the control systems by which man has changed natural resources into useful goods.*

Mankind has had the temerity to disregard the supreme life-force in relations with nature, substituting natural science for the rules of nature, and treating the natural environment as an inexhaustible reservoir of resources, and plundering resources in order to achieve a maximum material satisfaction, thus causing widespread environmental disruption and upsetting the balance between man and nature in the ecological sense.

Synergistic Feedforward and Globalism

In the information society, a new type of feedforward —synergistic— will come into being.

To support this synergistic feedforward in information society *the first* factor will be globalism. The spirit of globalism will establish the importance of the symbiosis of man and nature, and with the change in the spirit of the times will come the conception of ecological systems which harmonize the systems of nature and of humans to maintain and develop the existence of humanity.

The second factor is that the structure of the information productive power of computer communications technology has always had the characteristic of synergistic feedforward. Information does not disappear with use, and no matter how many times it is used its existence continues unchanged. Another point is that the structure of production is characterized by man-machine self-multiplication of information. Public usage and the synergistic feedforward of information both result from these two characteristics of the utility of computer-communications information; and further, the utility of information will become more and more oriented toward the public interest because of the great number of people who are able to use it.

In the information society of the future, *the right of usage* is predominant, not the right of ownership, and the principle of synergy rather than the principle of competition will be a basic societal principle.

This explains how synergistic feedforward will become a new type of feedforward system in the information society. In the future information society individuals will have a common social goal, and as individuals and groups, will build an order of social action among themselves in order to attain their goal by working together synergistically.

The first basic characteristic of this synergistic feedforward will be *the common goal*, based on common awareness and common group needs that do not conflict with the goals of individuals. *The second* is that action will be *voluntary*. There must be no coercion. *The third* is that individuals and groups will *cooperate actively* to attain their common goal, cooperation that will be dynamic, not static, in methods and organization. *The fourth* characteristic is *self-control*. Individuals and groups will voluntarily and continuously control their own action as they move toward the common goal. These are the basic principles of synergistic feedforward.

In the information society, however, synergistic feedforward will function as a common system for all mankind in relations with nature, and in relations between humans within society. This is the concept of globalism and the spirit of synergism between the divine and the human that unifies two feedforward systems.

14
Voluntary Communities: Core of the Social Structure

Futurization: The Fundamental Pattern of Life

Let us pass now to the question of the social structure and system in the information society. I believe the core of the social structure of the information society will be *voluntary communities*. Voluntary communities will be *the form of society in which people, of their own choice, will participate in building a community by their own efforts.* The basic precondition for bringing about such voluntary communities is what I have called *futurization*. The word 'futurization' implies *actualizing the future, bringing it into reality.* Expressed metaphorically, it means *to paint a design on the invisible canvas of the future, and then to actualize the design.*

When actualizing one's own future becomes the basic pattern of life in the information society it will be an epochal stage in the development of human society. Qualitative change and development in human society has, until now, followed the development of societal productive power, which means material productive power, the life patterns of people having been oriented toward the expansion of material consumption. This is true of all former types of society; hunting, agricultural and industrial.

In the information society, however, societal productive power will mean information productive power. The expansion and spread of this information-productive power will be the stimulus to seek fulfilment of time needs rather than material needs, encouraging the adoption of time values, and a new mode of social action oriented toward the realization of future time value.

Individual Futurization Stage as the Starting Point

Let us start with futurization by people as individuals —*the individual futurization stage*— inspiring the initiation of voluntary communities. To realize the time value of one's own future time, each person sets the target, on the invisible canvas, of a desirable and feasible vision, and sets about the task of actualizing it. Having selected the most appropriate action, one then goes on to means-oriented action. This is the individual futurization stage.

This individual futurization implies, however, two self-contradictions; there is *the inevitable conflict with the futurization of others,* as well as the essentially limited scale of individual futurization. Individual futurization, though termed individual, will have to be carried out within the structure of society, and conflicts will always arise between the futurization of one individual and another.

Let us suppose one takes action toward a goal that conflicts with that of another, reducing thereby the probability of an individual attaining the set goal. If, in order to increase the probability of achievement, one tries to actualize futurization by relying wholly on one's own chosen means-oriented action, then *the scope and scale of futurization is so much less.* Such futurization becomes merely a Robinson Crusoe-like self-sufficient futurization.

Another contradiction in the transition from an industrial to an information society will be *the contradiction between employed labor and voluntary labor.* If, in order to have more free time for oneself a person decreases working hours to a minimum, then income from employment will decline as free time increases, and to the extent that income decreases, there will be a decrease of purchasing power for the essential means of futurization.

Reaching the Stage of Group Futurization

Because of the need to break free of the contradictions of individual futurization, *group futurization* will gradually develop. By group futurization we do not mean futurization as a group that over-rides the individual, but group futurization that begins only with individual futurization. This form of group futurization expands and develops individual futurization, a stage that can only come about when three conditions are met. *First,* group futurization must be in accord with the needs and direction of individual futurization, if not directly, then, at least, indirectly; *second,* participation in the group futurization must be voluntary, with no restrictions whatever placed on participation; *third,* individual social labor in group futurization must always be in the nature of voluntary labor, not as controlled labor.

When these three conditions are met, participation in group futurization will not conflict with the needs of one's own futurization, but one's own futurization design will be actualized within a much wider involvement in society.

Let us consider some examples of this type of group futurization. One such might be venture businesses with *a new type of management organization.* A number of people who share the same business goal, might, for example, get together and set up a business venture. With shared risk, each would become responsible in the activities of the enterprise for one's own particular field. One might undertake the responsibility of providing capital; another might contribute specialized knowledge and experience. Each would have equal rights of participants in management; income from the enterprise would be distributed according to the agreement between all members, and each would agree to share the responsibility in case of loss. The activity of such an enterprise would not result in a return in profits to those providing the capital, but rather, would result in the participation of all members in deciding how to use and distribute the net income. In this type of venture all positions would be decided by the agreement of all participants which means that even the chosen president would be subject to the authority of the whole group, and failure to improve the performance of the enterprise would mean dismissal from such office. And if, for example, it was found that working for the enterprise conflicted with one's individual futurization, leaving the enterprise freely would be the only option. To carry out the responsibilities undertaken for a fixed period with the agreement of all would be the prime duty of such a person, who would not be able to quit before the term of office ended. This would be a completely new form of enterprise, exemplifying the type of group futurization that could develop in the information society.

Another example could be group futurization in the public arena. Suppose a person wants to actualize the desire to enjoy cycling, for which action begins on making a public cycling path in the vicinity. Such action begins from one's own individual needs. Suppose there are other enthusiastic cycling fans in the locality, eager to have a public cycling course. The originator, together with the others may bear part of the burden of cost for the purchase of necessary materials and tools, and may give free time in constructing the cycling course.

Voluntary Communities Appear

Futurization begins with individual futurization, advances to group futurization, and when it develops to a certain stage, it goes on to develop into *the community futurization* stage, in the formation of voluntary communities.

Community futurization differs fundamentally from the earlier stage of group futurization, not in an increase in the number of people participating or in the complexity of its functions, but in that it has now taken on the character of a community. I would call a small social unit composed of a group that comes together through community futurization, a voluntary community.

The 'classical concept of community' that has come down to us refers to *a group of people who carry on life together with a common social solidarity.* Communities have had a long traditional history, the general form of which up till now has been that of the local community. Their fundamental characteristics have been (1) a homogeneous creed for day-to-day living, (2) indigenous, (3) isolated, (4) communal ownership of the means of sustaining life, and (5) group life. There has been a strong tendency for communities to share a common religion, to be other-worldly, and self-sufficient.

The voluntary communities that we are considering here have several basic features in common with traditional cooperative communities.

The first is that such communities will come about by *voluntary association and be self-made.* People will participate of their own free will and build such communities by their own efforts and labor.

The second feature will be *voluntary management.* This means that the people themselves will become the subject that maintains social order within the group to which they belong; and further, that, on principle, social order will be maintained by the self-discipline of the individuals and the group. Voluntary management here means that the community will not operate on a system of bureaucratic control.

The third feature will be a sense of mission. People will share the goals of the community, bound strongly to each other by a sense of mission, and mutual support in the actualization of future goals.

The fourth will be *synergism.* People who belong to the community will work together in a mutually complementary way to achieve a shared goal.

On the other hand, voluntary communities in the information society will have several novel characteristics that mark them as differing vitally from traditional cooperative communities.

The first such characteristic is that the voluntary community will become *the most important social organizational unit* of the information society.

There are some examples of communities that have been voluntarily planned and created. The Puritans fled from England to a new continent with visions of creating an ideal society; there was Robert Owen's agricultural community; in Japan before the war there was

Saneatsu Mushakoji's Atarashiimura - New Village; more recently there are communes in the United States set up by what were called 'hippies', and others. Few of these voluntary utopian communities developed or were able to survive for long.

But voluntary communities of the new age will not be simply unattainable utopias. They will have ample realistic possibilities of success. Citizens will have abundant free time and a high standard of living, and a high level of education. Their way of life will expand from material consumption to futurization, and the socio-economic environment will become very conducive to the fulfillment of their desires. It is at this stage that a synergetic economic system and participatory democracy will become a reality.

In this development, voluntary communities will become widespread rather than being limited to restricted areas, scattered and isolated; they will become the most important organized social units constituting the information society.

The second characteristic will be their concept of *information space*. In such voluntary communities, ties to a locality will not necessarily be a fundamental property of the community as they have been in the past, because the emphasis and binding force will be shared common ideas and goals.

Such a community, not being tied to one locality, is a community that has information space, *invisible but perceptible space functionally bound together by information networks* based on computer communications technology. People belonging to such a community will work together in a mutually complementary way to achieve a shared goal. This emphasizes the strong sense of mission that unites them in seeking the goals of a community, the unity of a people bound strongly to each other by this sense of mission.

In referring to a 'community of destiny' I present *the idea of globalism*, the concept of this spaceship earth, on which alone makind can exist, and to *the common awareness* of the succession of crises confronting humanity; the population explosion, shortages of resources, the possibility of nuclear war, racism, the third world, and widespread poverty and hunger.

Even the roles of individuals will not be subdivided and separated into divisions of labor, as of now, but will take shape as *functional cooperative labor,* with roles changing dynamically in response to the changes in the environmental conditions surrounding the community. The people who make up such communities will need to be able to change their roles in response to current demands, and the assignment of new tasks within the community as a whole. Their functionally cooperative labor which dynamically changes will become the basis of societal development of such voluntary communities.

The third characteristic will be *the growth of multi-centered, multi-layered communities,* not as closed self-contained cooperative communities, but as *open* communities. Each community, while maintaining its independence, will be interlinked to complement other communities. More than that; groups and individuals making up each community will at the same time be participants in other communities, so that even moving to another community will be possible. It would be impossible for participants always to base their whole lives on one voluntary community, and freedom to seek income from other community sources or from general employment would be necessary. In other words, being a member of a functional voluntary community would not prevent a person from belonging to several communities or engaging in some other paying work.

So, generally speaking, citizens who are members of voluntary communities will belong as well to other social groups, thus being multi-belonging citizens. This is what we mean by multi-polar, multi-layered communities.

Seen in the macro sense, multi-layered voluntary communities will form an important societal sector operating alongside existing business and governmental sectors, and open to the two other sectors, maintaining mutually dependent relations with them, actively influencing them and ultimately bringing them into homogeneous relations.

The business sector, by establishing *mutually dependent relations with the voluntary sector,* will cease to be a self-sufficient and closed traditional sector, and will become the subject of vigorous development. In the transition from the industrial society to the information society, a high level of material productive capacity of the business sector will have to be maintained, but a fundamental change will take place in the nature, functions and role of the business sector, all basic industries taking on the form of public infrastructures. Further, *participation by the citizens in the management of enterprises* and *autonomous worker control* will become the pattern of management, and the managers will be trained experts in enterprise management.

The governmental sector will be greatly *simplified,* exercising a minimum of powers compared with the present aggrandized bureaucratic governmental organizations, all important policies of the state being decided by direct participation of the citizens. The dominant form of maintenance of public order replacing resort to the law, will be *the autonomous restraints exercized by the citizens themselves.*

Such changes in the business and government sectors are the outcome of the homogeneity developed with the voluntary sector.

When these sectors have become homogeneous with the voluntary sector, and the voluntary sector has become the leading societal form, human society will have been converted into a voluntary civil society, which is what we mean by *the high mass futurization society.*

Voluntary communities can be divided broadly into two types; *the local voluntary community,* and *the informational voluntary community.*

The Local Voluntary Community

This type of voluntary community will come into being in a specific locality, a new development along the line of existing types of local communities. A prototype of these local voluntary communities is already evidenced by the growth of citizens' movements.

If we regard consumer movements for *self-protection* against defective products as *the first* stage of citizens' movements, *the second* stage may be seen as citizens' movements centering on *anti-*pollution *campaigns* and *litigation*; and *the third* stage may be seen as *citizen participation in local government* by voluntary citizens' movements. These citizens' movements of the third stage can be seen as nascent prototypes of the local voluntary community. Quantitative changes take place in citizens movements belonging to the third category, a development from previous citizen movements, from protectionist activities that carry on campaigns, demonstrations, strikes, etc. to independent movements organized by the citizens themselves. At this third stage, active citizen movements, by *the voluntary efforts of the citizens* themselves, will set out to move their own civic life in the direction they desire. The autonomous productive activities that the residents in a given locality carry on for themselves, including farm production and cultivation by people living in public housing, managing for themselves the roads, parks, etc. in the area where they live, the delivery of newspapers and mail by the youth and students in the locality, and even the disposal treatment of garbage; all such activities will develop into full scale town planning, and the construction of a new community by the residents themselves.

The ultimate stage will involve voluntary management of the community. In this *fourth* stage the management of the local community will be by *the voluntary services of the citizens themselves.* The administration of law and justice over the nation and the state will be *greatly simplified,* and a complete decision of powers, with reduced functions of the central administration, will result. It will mean that the substance of local community operations will be concentrated into *smaller societies, each with its own characteristics and individuality.*

There will be communities of the elderly, communities of scientists, and idealistic and religious communities bound together by a common ideal or religion. Probably many other kinds of diverse local communities will evolve, such as communities of sunlovers or nature lovers.

The Informational Voluntary Community

The fundamental characteristic of such voluntary communities will be their freedom from ties to a local place, a completely new type of voluntary community. The fundamental bond to bring and bind people together will be *their common philosophy* and goals in day-to-day life; it is the technological base of *computer communications networks* that will make this possible. Communities formed in this way can be described as functional information space connected by information networks.

The precursor to these voluntary communities will be *the voluntary association[23]*, a social group voluntarily formed by people who have similar hobbies, beliefs, or ideals. There are many examples of such voluntary associations in current industrial society. We know one such as the Club of Rome, international in scope, and policy oriented. To be *international and policy oriented* is one of the fundamental characteristics of the voluntary communities that will emerge in the information society, because the very framework of the information society is globalism, the prevailing thought of our times; global information networks, and *a goal-oriented knowledge-creating citizenship.*

The Club of Rome, as a voluntary global knowledge-creating group, has wielded a strong influence on all people throughout the world, but it has not yet escaped from the restrictions of a voluntary association. Many more conditions must evolve before this kind of association can develop into a voluntary community. Global information networks have only just come into being, and these are used for stage goals by big countries such as European, the United States and the Soviet Union, and civilian use has not progressed beyond the large multi-national corporations, nor have the citizens of the current mass society developed such attitudes as will be necessary for the formation of a informational community; and further, this kind of international, policy-oriented informational community can only come into being when many voluntary communities (small social groups) have already been formed and have linked up in various ways.

To take as an example of this sort of global, informational, voluntary community of the future, we can imagine what we now call *a zero population informaional community.*

Population control will be an essential means of saving mankind from endemic hunger and poverty such as we see in some places now, and which could become global by a world-wide population explosion. It is a situation calling for an informational community organized by people throughout the world to set this problem and goal before all people. The program of action would be something like *'no family to consist of more than two children',* an ideal actually followed by the families of those participating in such a community. It is important to note that this form of population control will not be by the enforcement of laws and the authority of the state, but by *emulation and voluntary self-control exercised by families and individuals.* To exercise birth control, the member groups would provide publicity, counseling, medical care, and the best hospital equipment. The necessary funds to carry this out will be provided by *the contributions of individual members,* by business circles and by governmental aid where necessary.

Some additional points need to be mentioned here. Those who voluntarily participate in the zero population movement will naturally observe the standards set on ideal family size. Then, too, part of one's ability, income, and time, will be devoted to the movement, with activities of individual participants carried out voluntarily, and independent of government policy, laws, funds and facilities. The accumulative result of this kind of communal action will be a decisive factor in curbing any population explosion, one of mankind's major problems.

My own firm belief is that many such global informational voluntary communities will take shape as we approach the twenty-first century.

Among such, the most needed and feasible communities would be 'non-smoking voluntary communities,'[24]'global anti-nuclear weapon, complete disarmament communities,' 'global energy conservation and anti-pollution, nature preservation communities.'

Globalism, time value, and a goal oriented mode of action will be the universal concepts we share in these global voluntary communities.

People, while individually pursuing their own futualization needs through goal-oriented action will participate and work together in one or more voluntary communities, and as members of a global community, will cooperate in solving the problems and crises that are common to all mankind.

This is how I see the future information society ultimately functioning.

15
Computopia: Rebirth of Theological Synergism

A Vision of Computopia

As I come to the final chapters of this book about the information society, I want to round off my discussion with *A Vision of Computopia* (abbreviation of Computer utopia)[15]. Looking back over the history of human society, we see that as the traditional society of the Middle Ages was drawing to a close, the curtain was rising on the new industrial society. Thomas More, Robert Owen, Saint Simon, Adam Smith and other prophets arose with a variety of visions portraying the emerging society. The one that is of special interest to me is Adam Smith's vision of *a universal opulent society,* [26] which he sets out in 'The Wealth of Nations.' Smith's universal affluent society conceives the condition of plenty for the people, economic conditions that should free the people from dependence and subordination, and enable them to exercise true independence of spirit in autonomous actions.

Smith presented The Wealth of Nations to the world in 1776. Strangely, James Watt's first steam engine was completed in the same year, but although the Industrial Revolution was under way, Smith's grand vision of a universal society of plenty was still far off when he died in 1790. His vision seems to be half-realized two centuries later, as society reaches Rostow's High Mass Consumption stage.[27] The High Mass Consumption stage means that the material side of Smith's vision of people having material wealth in plenty is partially accomplished, at least in the advanced countries. The wider vision he had of individual independence and autonomy that would follow has clearly not been realized, because the axis around which the mass production and consumption of industrial goods turns in industrial society comprises machines and power. Capital investments are necessarily immense, with the result that the concentration of capital and corresponding centralized power are the dominating factors. This is the fundamental structure of all industrial societies, something that transcends the question of a society being capitalistic or socialistic.

Industrial societies are characterized by centralized government supported by a massive military and administrative bureaucracy, and in capitalist states supra-national enterprises have been added that make the modern state dependent on the trinity of industry, the military, and the government bureaucracy. In industrial societies the individual has freedom to take social action in three ways. A person is able to participate indirectly in government policy by voting in elections once every few years. One has the freedom of using income (received as compensation for subsistence labor) to purchase food and other articles necessary to sustain life, which implies freedom to use free time on weekends and holidays as one likes. This freedom of selection, however, is freedom only in a limited sense, quite removed from the voluntary action selection that Adam Smith envisioned.

As the 21st century approaches, however, the possibilities of a universally opulent society being realized have appeared in the sense that Smith envisioned it, and the information society (futurization society) that will emerge from the computer communications revolution will be a society that actually moves toward a universal society of plenty.

The most important point I would make is that the information society will *function around the axis of information values rather than material values,* cognitive and action-selective information. In addition, the information utility, the core organization for the production of information, will have the fundamental character of an infrastructure, and knowledge capital will predominate over material capital in the structure of the economy.

Thus, if industrial society is *a society in which people have affluent material consumption,* the information society will be *a society in which the cognitive creativity of individuals flourishes throughout society.* And if the highest stage of industrial society is the high mass consumption society, then the highest stage of the information society will be *the global futurization society,* a vision that greatly expands and develops Smith's vision of a universal opulent society; this is what I mean by 'Computopia'. This global futurization society will be a society in which everyone pursues the possibilities of one's own future, actualizing one's own self-futurization needs by acting in a goal-oriented way. It will be *global, in which multi-centered voluntary communities of citizens participating voluntarily in shared goals and ideas flourish simultaneously throughout the world.*

Computopia is a wholly new long-term vision for the 21st century, bearing within it the following seven-fold concepts:

Pursuit and Realization of Time-Value

My first vision of Computopia is that it will be *a society in which each individual pursues and realizes time-value.* In Japan, the advanced welfare society is often talked about, and people are now calling for a shift of emphasis from rapid economic growth to stable growth, stressing social welfare and human worth, sometimes expressed as a shift from a GNP society to a GNW society, i.e. gross national welfare. The current idea of an advanced welfare society, however, tends to place the emphasis on the importance of living in a green environment where the sun shines. Obviously, in seeking to escape from the pollution and congestion of cities, and from the threat of a controlled society, this concept is significant, as indicative of our times. Yet it does not embrace a dynamic vision of the future, which I feel is its greatest weakness. The disappearance of pollution and congestion or even escape from the cities will not alone bring satisfaction. Human needs are of a very high dimension that must be actively satisfied, the need for self-realization. The futurization society, as I see it, will be a society in which each individual is able to pursue and satisfy the need for self-fulfillment.

The self-realization I refer to is nothing less than the need to realize time value, and time value, of course, involves painting one's own design on the invisible canvas of one's future, and then setting out to create it. Such self-fulfillment will not be limited merely to individuals all pursuing their own self-realization aims, but will expand to include mini-groups, local societies, and functional communities.

Freedom of Decision and Equality of Opportunity

My *second* vision is *freedom of decision and equality of opportunity.* The concepts of freedom and equality grew out of the Puritan Revolution (1649—1660) which occurred in England around the end of the Middle Ages. Initially the ideas of *freedom from absolute authority* and *legal equality* underlay these concepts, backed by the theories of social contract and individual consent as the basis of political authority, theories that maintain that freedom and equality are natural rights for all people. These two ideas provided the theoretical base for the formation of modern civil society.

As the capitalist economic system came into being, freedom and equality developed conceptually to include 'freedom to work at something of one's own choice', 'equality of ownership'. and 'freedom to select an occupation,' and 'industrial equality,' more commonly referred to as free competition.

The information society will offer new concepts of freedom and equality, embodying *freedom of decision* and *equality of opportunity*.

As I have said, the information society will be a society in which each individual pursues and realizes time value. In this type of society the freedom that an individual will want most will be *freedom to determine voluntarily the direction of time value realization in the use of available future time*. Call it 'freedom of decision.' Freedom of decision is the freedom of decision-making for selection of goal-oriented action, and refers to the right of each individual to voluntarily determine how to use future time in achieving a goal. This will be the most fundamental human right in the future information society.

'Equality of opportunity' is *the right that all individuals must have, meaning that the conditions and opportunities for achieving the goals they have set for themselves must be available to them.* This will guarantee that all individuals have complete equality in all opportunities for education, and the opportunity to utilize such opportunities for action selection. Guaranteed equality of opportunity will, for the first time, assure that the people will share equally the maximum opportunities for realizing time value.

Flourishing Diverse Voluntary Communities

My *third* vision is that there will be a *flourishing of diverse voluntary communities*. A society composed of highly educated people with a strong sense of community has long been a dream of mankind, and several attempts have been made to bring it into being. Recently communes have been formed by young groups, and a number of cooperative communities have been formed in Japan. One was the *Yamagishi-kai*, formed after the war. The rapid growth of information productive power built around the computer will see some big advances and developments beyond the ideas and attempts of the past. There will be enhanced independence of the individual, made possible for the first time by the high level of the information productive power of the information society. The development of information productive power will liberate man by reducing dependence on subsistence labor, with rapidly increasing material productive power as the result of automation, thus increasing the amount of free time one can use. There will also be an expanded ability to solve problems and pursue new possibilities, and then to bring such possibilities into reality; that is to say, it will expand one's ability for futurization.

The development of this information productive power will offer the individual more independence than can be enjoyed now.

Another point to be noted is the autonomous expansion of creativity that will follow. The keynote of utopian societies in the past has been the establishment of communal life through the common ownership of the means of production, based more or less on the prototype of primitive communism. This type of society has inevitably operated with a relatively low level of productive power; but the future information society will ensure more active voluntary communities, because humans will be liberated from dependence on subsistence labor, and because of the expanded possibilities for future time-value realization.

As a consequence, utopian societies will move on from being merely cooperative societies, where most time must still be given to sustaining existence, to become dynamic and creative voluntary communities. It is people with common goals who will form the new voluntary communities, communities that will always be carried on by voluntary activity and the creative participation of individuals; individual futurization and group futurization will be harmoniously co-ordinated with societal futurization. In the mature information society of the future, nature communities, non-smoking communities, energy conservation communities, and many other new types of voluntary communities will prosper side by side.

Interdependent Synergistic Societies

My *fourth* vision is *the realization of interdependent synergistic societies.* A synergistic society is one that develops as individuals and groups cooperate in complementary efforts to achieve the common goals set by the society as a whole. The functioning societal principle is *synergism,* a new principle to replace the free competition of the current capitalistic society.

In the future information society, information utilities, whose structure of production is characterized by self-multiplication and synergy, will take the place of the present large factories, and become the societal symbol of the information society. These information utilities will be the centers of productive power, yielding time value that will be the common goal of voluntary communities, because of *the self-multiplication* that characterized production in the information utility. Unlike material goods, information does not disappear by being consumed, and even more important, the value of information can be amplified indefinitely by constant additions of new information to the existing information. People will thus continue to utilize information which they and others have created even after it has been used, and, at macro level, the most effective way to increase the production and utilization of information will be for *people to work together to make and share societal information.* This economic rationality means that the information utility itself will become part of the infrastructure. It will be the force behind the productive power which gives birth to socio-economic values, and corresponding new socio-economic laws and systems will come into being as a matter of course. *Synergistic feedforward* will function as the new societal principle to establish and develop social order, with the resulting societies becoming voluntary communities.

Functional Societies Free of Overruling Power

My *fifth* vision is of *the realization of functional societies free of overruling power.* The history of the rule of man over man is long, continuing right into the present, simply changing form from absolute domination by an aristocracy linked with religion in feudal society to economic domination of enterprises in capitalist society, and to political domination by the bureaucracy in both socialist and capitalist society. The future information society, however, will become a *classless society,* free of overruling power, the core of society being voluntary communities. This will begin as informational and local communities comprising a limited number of people steadily develop and expand. A voluntary community is a society in which the independence of the individual harmonizes with the order of the group, and the social structure is a multi-centered structure characterized by mutual cohesion. By 'multi-centered' I mean that *every individual and group in a voluntary community is independent, and becomes a center.'* Mutual cohesion' means that *both individuals and groups that constitute the centers share a mutual attraction to form a social group.* Behind this mutual attraction lies the common goal, the spirit of synergy, with the ethics of self-imposed restraints. In other words, as individuals pursue their own time value, they work synergetically as a group to achieve a shared goal, and all exercise self-restraint so that there will be no interference with the social activities of others. This social structure is the overall control system of a voluntary community. In the political system, democracy based on participation of the citizens will be the general mode of policy making, rather than the indirect democracy of the parliamentary system. The technological base to support this participatory democracy will consist of (1) information networks made possible by the development of computer-communications technology, (2) simulation of policy models, and (3) feedback loops of individual opinions;

with the result that policy making will change from policy making based on majority versus minority rule to policy making based on the balance of gain and loss to individuals in the spectrum of their areas of concern, both in the present and in future time. In policy making by this means, the feedback and accumulation of opinions will be repeated many times until agreement is reached, to insure the impartial balance of merits and demerits of the policy decision as it affects individuals and groups with conflicting interests.

The present bureaucratic administrative organization will be converted into *a voluntary management system of the citizens.* Only a small staff of specialists will be needed to carry out administrative duties, officers who are really professionals responsible for the administrative functions. The bureaucratic organization of a privileged class will disappear. In this voluntary civil society, ruling, coercion, and control over others will cease. Society will be *synergistically functional,* the ideal form that the information society should take.

Computopia: Can It Become a Reality?

Can these visions of Computopia be turned into reality? We cannot escape the need to choose, before it is established, either 'Computopia' or an 'Automated State'. These inescapable alternatives present two sharply contrasting bright and dark pictures of the future information society. If we choose the former, the door to a society filled with boundless possibilities will open; but if the latter, our future society will become a horrible and forbidding age.

As far as present indications go, we can say that there is *a considerable danger that we may move toward a controlled society.*

This is seen in the following tendencies:

During the first fifteen to twenty years of their availability, computers were used mainly by the military and other government organizations and large private institutions. Medium and small enterprises and individuals were generally barred from using computer-communications technology, since large scale computers at the early stages of automation were extremely costly. This situation caused a significant delay in democratic applications of computers. Initially, computers were used mainly for automatic control and labor-saving purposes, rather than 'problem-solving' applications. The development of automatic control of separate systems to integrated real-time control systems covering broad areas is increasing the danger of a controlled society.

The utilization of computers for major scientific and technological applications, such as space development, has led us to neglect the need for coexistence with nature, while our impact on nature has grown immeasurably. The development of 'big' science and technology has operated in such a way as to further increase the imbalance between human and nature systems.

If computerization continues in this direction, the possibility of a controlled society increases alarmingly.

However, I believe and predict that *the catastrophic course to an 'Automated State' will be avoided,* and that our choice will be to follow the path to 'Computopia.' I give you two logical reasons for my confidence.

The first theoretical basis is that *the computer as innovational technology is an ultimate science.* By 'ultimate science' I mean *a science that will bring immeasurable benefits to humanity if wisely used, but which would lead to destruction if used wrongly.* Nuclear energy, for example, can be an extremely useful source of energy, but it could kill the greater part of the human race in an instant. The computer may, in one sense, be more important, as an ultimate science, than atomic energy.

If computers were to be used exclusively for automation, a controlled society, the alienation of mankind and social decadence would become a reality. But if used fully for the creation of knowledge, a high mass knowledge creation society will emerge in which all people will feel their lives to be worth living. Further, an on-line, real-time system of computers connected to terminals with communication lines would turn society into a thoroughly managed society if utilized in a centralized way, but if their utilization is decentralized and open to all persons, it will lead to creation of a high mass knowledge creation society. Similarly, if data banks were to be utilized by a small group of people in power to serve their political purposes, it would become a police state, but if used for health control and career development, every person can be saved from the sufferings of disease, and be enabled to develop full potentialities, opening up new future opportunities and possibilities.

The computer thus confronts us with these alternatives: An "Automated State" or a "Computopia." So it is *not the forecasting* of the state of a future information society, *but our own choice* that is decisive. There is only one choice for us —the road to computopia. We cannot allow the computer, an ultimate science, to be used for the destruction of the spiritual life of mankind.

The second theoretical basis of my confidence is that *the information society will come about through a systematic, orderly transformation.* The information society will be such that information productive power will develop rapidly to replace material productive power, a development that will bring about a qualitative conceptual change in production, from production of material goods to the production of systems. What I mean is the production of far-reaching systems that include everything from production systems for material goods (such as automated factories), to social systems (wired cities, self-education systems), to political systems (direct citizen participation systems), and even to ecological systems.

Obviously, information productive power centering on the computer communications network will be the powerful thrust to bring about societal systems innovations. New social and economic systems will be created continuously, and society as a whole will undergo dynamic changes, not the drastic social changes of the past, typified by the power struggles of ruling classes, wars between nation states, and the political revolutions of mass revolt. It will be achieved through *systematic, orderly transformation.* As old socio-economic systems gradually become ineffectual and unable to meet the needs of the times, they will atrophy, and new, responsive socio-economic systems will take their place, in the way that a metamorphosis takes place with an organism, the useless parts of the body atrophying and other parts developing in response to the new demands.

Moreover, this systematic transformation of the societal structure will be brought about by citizen action, *changing means-and-goal oriented modes of action into cause-and-effect modes of action.* I have pointed out that human modes of action will become goal-oriented in the information society. These modes of goal-oriented action will evolve to the point where they function as a goal principle, to become the principle of social action. When this happens, social action will be logical, means-oriented action for the pursuit of common goals. So we can replace the term, 'goal-means oriented action,' with the term, 'cause-effect relationship,' following the idea of Max Weber, who changed this concept of goal-means relationship into a concept of cause-effect relationship. In the information society, the social actions of citizens in general will become goal-means relationships that operate as cause-effect relationships.

The Rebirth of Theological Synergism of Man and the Supreme Being

The final goal of Computopia is *the rebirth of theological* synergism of man and the supreme being, or if one prefers it, the ultimate life force, expressions that have meaning both to those of religious faith and the irreligious. This can be called the ultimate goal of Computopia. The relation existing between man and nature was the beginning of civilization. For many thousands of years man was completely encompassed by the systems of nature, which he had to obey or be destroyed by them. Five or six thousand years ago, man succeeded in harnessing these systems of nature in a limited way to increase agricultural production, and the first civilizations were built. This marked the beginning of man's conquest of nature. But with the Industrial Revolution the conquest of nature meant the destruction of nature, and now nature's retaliation has begun, the sequel to man's relation with nature that turned into destruction.

Now, a new relationship is beginning. At last, man and nature have begun to act together in a new ecological sense, on a global scale, in synergistic society. At the base of this conversion of human society into an ecological system is the awareness of the limitations of scientific technology. It means awareness that scientific technology is simply the application of scientific principles, and that these can not be changed by man, nor can he create new principles to work and live by. It is also a new awareness of the commonality of man's destiny, in that there is no place where man can live except on this earth, which first gave him life; from this very awareness is emerging the idea of a synergistic society where man and nature must exist in true symbiosis.

This is the assertive, dynamic idea that *man can live and work together with nature, not by a spirit of resignation that says man can only live within the framework of natural systems;* but, not living in hostility to nature, man and nature will work together as one. Put another way, man approaches the universal supra life, with man and god acting as one.

God does not refer to a god in the remote heavens; it refers to nature with which we live our daily lives. The scientific laws that we have already identified and are aware of are simply manifestations of the activity of this supreme power. The ultimate ideal of the global futurization society will be for man's actions to be in harmony with nature in building a synergistic world.

This synergism is a modern rebirth of the theological synergism which teaches that *'spiritual rebirth depends upon the cooperation of the will of man and the grace of God,'* however it may be expressed. It aims to build an earthly, not a heavenly, synergistic society of god and man.

When we open the book of history, we see that when man brought about the accumulation of wealth and an increase in productive power, various choices had to be made. The Greeks built magnificent temples to Apollo and carved beautiful statues of Venus. The Egyptians built gigantic pyramids for their Pharaohs, and the Romans turned the brutalities of the Colosseum into a religious rite. The

Chinese built the Great Wall to keep out the barbarians. Now man has made the fires of heaven his own, and left footprints on the craters of the moon.

We are moving toward the 21st century with the very great goal of building a Computopia on earth, the historical monument of which will be only several chips one inch square in a small box. But that box will store many historical records, including the record of how four billion world citizens overcame the energy crisis and the population explosion; achieved the abolition of nuclear weapons and complete disarmament; conquered illiteracy; and created a rich symbiosis of god and man without the compulsion of power or law, but by the voluntary cooperation of the citizens to put into practice their common global aims.

Accordingly, the civilization to be built as we approach the 21st century will not be a material civilization symbolized by huge constructions, but will be virtually *an invisible civilization*. Precisely, it should be called an 'information civilization.' *Homo sapiens,* who stood at the dawn of the first material civilization at the end of the last glacial age, is now standing at the threshold of the second, the information civilization after ten thousand years.

References

1. H.A. Simon, *'The Impact of the Computer on Management'*, Presented at the 15th CIOS World Conference, Tokyo, Japan, 1969.
2. Y. Masuda, *'A New Development Stage of the Information Revolution'*, Applications of Computer/Communications Systems, DECD Informatics Studies 8. Paris: DECD, 1975.
   The Plan for Information Society: A National Goal toward the 2000 Year. Tokyo: Japan Computer Usage Development Institute, 1971.
3. *Toward the Information Society.* Report of the Industrial Structure Council, Ministry of International Trade and Industry. Tokyo: Computer Age, 1969.
4. *The International Opinion Poll on 'The Plan for Information Society.* JCUDI Report, Tokyo: Japan Computer Usage Development Institute, 1973.
5. *Report on Tama CCIS Experiment Project in Japan.* Tokyo: Living-Visual Information System Development Association, 1978.
6. *Report on Hi-OVIS Experiment Project.* Tokyo: Living-Visual Information System Development Association, 1979.
7. J.C. Madden, *Videotex in Canada.* Ottawa: Department of Communications, Government of Canada, 1979.
8. *Telecommunications and Regional Development in Sweden.* Stockholm: A Progress Report of Swedish Board for Technical Development, 1977.
9. Y. Masuda, *'Social Impact of Computerization. An Application of the Pattern Model for Industrial Society,* Challenges from the Future. Tokyo: Kodansha, 1970.
10. Y. Masuda, *'The Conceptual Framework of Information Economics,* IEEE Transaction on Communications, October 1975. New York: IEEE Communications Society.
11. S. Kuznets, *Modern Economic Growth: Rate, Structure and Spread.* New Hayen and London: Yale University Press, 1966.

12. J. Ota, *Amoeba,* NHK Books. Tokyo: Nihon Hoso Shuppan Kyokai, 1960.
13. Y. Masuda, '*Computopia vs. Automated States: Unavoidable Alternatives for the Information Era*' The Next 25 Years, Crisis and Opportunity. Washington D.C.: World Future Society, 1975.
14. K.E. Boulding, *The Economy of Love and Fear: A Preface to Grants Economics.* California: Wadsworth, 1973.
15. Y. Masuda, '*Triple Concept of Information Economics*', Proceedings of the 2nd International Conference on Computer Communication, Stockholm, 1974.
16. Y. Masuda, '*Future Perspectives for Information Utility*', Proceedings of the International Conference on Computer Communication, Kyoto, Japan, 1978
17. Y. Masuda, '*A New Era of Global Information Utility*', Proceedings of Eurocomp 78, London, 1978.
18. Y. Masuda, *Information Economics.* Tokyo: Sangyo Noritsu University Press, 1976.
19. Y. Masuda, '*Privacy in the Future Information Society*', Computer Networks, Special Issue, 1979. Amsterdam: North-Holland.
20. Y. Masuda, '*Management of Information Technology for Developing Countries: Adaptation of Japanese Experience to Developing Countries*', Data Exchange, April 1974. London: Diebold Europe.
21. Y. Masuda, '*A Plan for the Information Society in Developing Countries*', Presentation at the 5th Brazil Telecommunication Congress, Sao Paulo, 1979.
22. H. Otsuka, *Method of Social Science.* Tokyo: Iwanami Publishing Co., 1966.
23. W.M. Kitzmiller, R. Ottinger, *Citizen Action: Vital Force for Change.* Washington D.C.: Center for a Voluntary Society, 1971.
24. *Aktuellt,* Bulletin of VISIR. Stockholm: VISIR. The Smoking Digest: Progress Report on a Nation Kicking the Habit. Washington D.C.: US Department of Health, Education, and Welfare, 1977.
25. Y. Masuda, *Computopia.* Tokyo: Diamond, 1966.
26. A. Smith, '*An Early Drft of the Wealth of Nations*' in W.R. Scott, Adam Smith as Student and Professor. Glasgow: 1937.
27. W.W. Rostow, *The Stage of Economic Growth.* London: The Syndics of the Cambridge University Press, 1960.

Glossary

affective information: information that is based on sensitivity and production of emotion. It embraces all the information that conveys sensory feelings, such as 'comfort,' 'pain' and the emotional feelings of 'happy' and 'sad.'

arts industries: the industries that process, retrieve and service affective information or produce and sell related equipment. See **affective information, information industries.**

balanced feedforward: the subject of action and the external environment exercise mutual control if their relations are in balance. See **feedforward.**

CAI: computer aided instruction, computer-oriented self-learning system.

cognitive information: information that is a projection of the future; it is logical and action-selective. The projection means that the cognitive information is used for detecting and forecasting.

Computopia: Computer utopia, an ideal global society in which multi-centered, multi-layered voluntary communities of citizens participating voluntarily in shared goals and ideas flourish simultaneously throughout the world. See **voluntary community.**

controlled feedforward: the subject of action controls the external environment in the feedforward process. See **feedforward.**

CVS: computer controlled vehicle system, a transportation network in a new town, with automatically controlled passenger cars on rails, each designed to carry four persons.

dependent feedforward: the subject of action dependent on the eternal environment in the feedforward process. See **feedforward.**

environmental information: information concerned with relation between an organism and the external world in order to maintain its existence. See **organismic information.**

ethics industries: the industries that process, retrieve and service ethical information.

feedfoward: control in moving toward a goal, and viewed from the standpoint of the subject of action, it means a controlled development of the current situation to change it to a more desirable situation. See **dependent**

feedforward, controlled feedforward, balanced feedforward, synergistic feedforward.

field: the space with concrete content within which the subject of action acts with conscious purpose. See **subject of action, process.**

futurization: future actualization; this implies actualizing the future, bringing it into reality. Expressed metaphorically, it means to paint a design on the invisible canvas of the future, and then to actualize the design.

GIU: global information utility, a global information infrastructure using a combination of computers, communication networks and satellites. See **information utility.**

Hi-Ovis: Higashi-Ikoma Optical Visual Information System, the first major experiment of its kind, a future living visual information city, in that it utilizes optical fiber cable instead of copper cable for two-way multiplex communication of video and audio signals and data.

historical analogy: societal foreseeing approach based on historical hypothesis; the past developmental pattern of human society can be used as a historical analogical model for future society.

information: an informed situational relation between a subject and an object that makes possible the action selection by which the subject itself can achieve some sort of use value. See **affective information, cognitive information.**

informational voluntary communities: a completely new type of voluntary community. It is the technological base of computer communications networks that will make this possible. See **voluntary communities.**

information cycle: informative cycle of subject-object-signal-action. The subject receives a signal from the object, identifies the signal and evaluates it according to an acquired standard of judgement, selects a course of action, and finally achieves some use value by implementing the action.

information epoch: the span of time during which there is an innovation in information technology that becomes the latent power of societal transformation that can bring about an expansion in the quantity and quality of information and a large-scale increase in the stock of information.

information gap: the relative absense of information processing and transmission technology between industrialized and developing countries, to which must be added the human factors of levels of intellectual development and behavioral patterns in such countries.

IIO: International Information Organization.

information industries: the industries that process, retrieve and service cognitive information, or produce and sell related equipment. See **knowledge industries.**

information society: a society that grows and develops around information, and brings about a general flourishing state of human intellectual creativity, instead of affluent material consumption.

information space: the field provided within the new space, which is connected with the networks of information, characterized by two features: 1) it does not have boundaries like a territorial field and 2) in this field, elements related by objective-oriented action are related to each other through information networks.

information utility: an information infrastructure consisting of public information processing and service facilities that combine computer and communication networks. From these facilities anyone anywhere at any time will be able easily, quickly, and inexpensively to get any information which one wants to get.

knowledge: cognitive information that has been generalized and abstracted from an understanding of the cause- and effect-relations of a particular phenomenon occuring in the external environment. See **information, cognitive information, technology.**

knowledge industries: the industries that produce, sell service knowledge and knowledge related equipment. See **information industries.**

objectification of information: the separation of information from its subject.

opportunity development: research and development of possibilities of future time usage or creating new values in rapidly changing environmental conditions.

organismic information: information concerned with physiological functions to maintain life within the body of the organism. See **environmental information.**

participatory democracy: a form of government in which policy decisions both for the state and for local self-government bodies will be made through the participation of ordinary citizens.

problem solving: a method or means of eliminating risks that may stand in the way of accomplishing an aim.

Project TERESE: an experimental project of the Swedish government to analyse the possibilities of promoting desirable regional development by the use of telecommunications. This project is of special interest in relation to their theme of voluntary action and synergy.

Process: the development in time of a situation created artifically by the interaction between the purposeful action on the field of the subject of action and the reaction of the field to it. See **subject of action, field.**

quaternary industries: a new classification of industries; it is reasonable to distinguish information-related industries from service industries, and classify them as quaternary industries to provide a clear concept of the industrial structure of an information society.

situational reform: a process in which the current situation is changed into a new situation that is consistent with the subject's goal, as expressed by the following formula:

$$\text{Situation A} \rightarrow \text{Situation A'} \rightarrow \text{Realization of a value}$$

(Current situation)	(Desirable situation)	(Satisfaction of a want)

See **situational relation.**

self-multiplication of information: the quality of information is raised by adding new information of what has already been accumulated, and the accumulation of information leads to further accumulation of information which in turn means still further accumulation of information through time and space.

situational relation: the relation between a subject and an object that comes into being in a particular situation, and to which there are three conditions: (1) there must be a subject and an object (in this case the environment surrounding the subject), (2) the subject must receive impulses from the object, and (3) the subject takes action in response to these impulses. See **situational reform.**

societal technology: this technology has four fundamental characteristics: (1) many different kinds of innovational technology are joined together to constitute one complex system of technology, (2) these integrated systems of technology spread throughout society as a whole and gradually take root. (3) as a result, there occurs a rapid expansion of a new type of productivity, (4) the development of this new type of productivity has a societal impact great enough to bring about the transformation from traditional society to a new society.

subject of action: the subject which works on the field with objective-consciousness. Such may be any individual, group of individuals, or organizations engaging in social action with deliberate purpose. See **field, process.**

synergistic feedforward: the subject of action and the external environment are in mutually complementary relations and act together to reach a common objective.

synergy: a combined functional action by a group to achieve a common goal.

systems industries: the structure of the systems industries will consist of a complex of industries formed by linking up existing industries with the information industries.

Tama CCIS: Tama Coaxial Cable Information System; two-way community information systems which combine computers with up-to-date communications technology and can be considered as miniturized prototypes of the information society of the future.

Technology: cognitive information that is useful in effectively carrying out production-oriented labor requiring a certain degree of prescribed expertise. See **cognitive information, knowledge.**

TELIDON: an experimental project of Canadian government for videotex service.

TERESE: See **project TERESE.**

theological synergism: the assertive, dynamic idea that man can live and work together with nature, not by a spirit of resignation that says man can only live within the framework of natural systems; but, not living in hostility to nature, man and nature will work together as one. Put another way, man approaches the universal supra-life, with man and god acting as one.

time-value: the value which man creates in the purposeful use of future time. Put in more picturesque terms, man designs a goal on the invisible canvas of the future, and goes on to attain it.

time sharings system: the system by which several users have access to a computer simultaneously.

T.S.S.: See time sharing system.

voluntary community: a community in which a group of people carry on life together voluntarily with a common social solidarity. The fundamental bond to bring and bind people together will be their common philosophy and goals in day to day life. See **informational voluntary communities.**

Index

World Future Society
An Association for the Study of Alternative Futures

The World Future Society is an association of people who are interested in how social and technological developments will shape the future. It is chartered as a nonprofit scientific and educational organization in Washington, D.C., U.S.A.

The Society was founded in 1966 by a group of private citizens who felt that people need to anticipate coming developments to make wise personal and professional decisions. In our turbulent era of change, the Society strives to be an unbiased and reliable clearinghouse for a broad range of scholarly forecasts, analyses, and ideas.

As outlined in its charter, the Society's objectives are:

1. To contribute to a reasoned awareness of the future and of the importance of its study.

2. To advance responsible and serious investigation of the future.

3. To promote the development and improvement of methodologies for the study of the future.

4. To increase public understanding of future-oriented activities and studies.

5. To facilitate communication and cooperation among organizations and individuals interested in studying or planning for the future.

Since its inception, the Society has grown to include more than 40,000 members in over 80 countries. Society members come from all professions and have a wide range of interests, and the Society counts many distinguished scientists, businessmen, and government leaders among its ranks.

The Society publishes a number of future-oriented periodicals, including:

● THE FUTURIST: A Journal of Forecasts, Trends, and Ideas About the Future. This exciting bimonthly magazine, which is sent to all members, explores all aspects of the future—technology, life-styles, government, economics, values, environmental issues, religion, etc. Written in clear, informative prose by experts, THE FUTURIST gives every member an advance look at what may happen in the years ahead.

● *The World Future Society Bulletin.* This bimonthly journal is intended for professional futurists, forecasters, planners, and others with an intense interest in the field. The *Bulletin* carries articles on forecasting methods, news of special interest in the field, book reviews, etc.

● *Future Survey* is a monthly abstract journal reporting on recent books and articles about the future. Each 16- to 24-page issue contains more than 100 summaries of the most significant futures-relevant literature.

Books published by the Society include *The Future: A Guide to Information Sources, The Study of the Future, Education and the Future,* and *The Information Society of Tomorrow.*

The Society's "bookstore of the future" stocks hundreds of books, and also a number of audiotapes, games, and films.

One of the principal activities of the World Future Society is the planning of a variety of futures conferences—both large and small—at which participants can exchange ideas and keep up to date on the latest futuristic developments in their field of interest. The Society's large General Assemblies have been held in Washington, D.C. (1971 and 1975) and in Toronto, Canada (1980); the Fourth General Assembly will be in Washington, D.C., July 18-22, 1982. The Society also has sponsored annual conferences on education (beginning in 1978) and special meetings on energy, business, and communications.

At the local level, the Society has active chapters in a growing number of cities scattered throughout the United States and around the world. These chapters offer speakers, educational courses, seminars, discussion groups, and other opportunities for members to get to know each other in their local communities.

Membership in the World Future Society is open to anyone seriously interested in the future. For further information, write to:

World Future Society
4916 St. Elmo Avenue
Bethesda, MD 20814, U.S.A.
Telephone: (301) 656-8274

World Future Society Publications

Cornish, Edward, ed. *The Future: A Guide to Information Sources.* Revised 2nd edition. Washington, D.C.: World Future Society. 1979. 722 pages. Paperback. $25.00. The revised and expanded second edition of this indispensable guide to the futures field contains even more information than the highly-praised first edition.

Cornish, Edward, ed. *1999: The World of Tomorrow.* Washington, D.C.: World Future Society. 1978. 160 pages. Paperback. $4.95. This first anthology of articles from THE FUTURIST is divided into four sections: "The Future as History," "The Future as Progress," "The Future as Challenge," and "The Future as Invention."

Cornish, Edward. *The Study of the Future: An Introduction to the Art and Science of Understanding and Shaping Tomorrow's World.* Washington, D.C.: World Future Society. 1977. 320 pages. Paperback. $9.50. A general introduction to futurism and future studies. Chapters discuss the history of the futurist movement, ways to introduce future-oriented thinking into organizations, the philosophical assumptions underlying studies of the future, methods of forecasting, current thinking about what may happen as a result of the current revolutionary changes in human society, etc. The volume also includes detailed descriptions of the lives and thinking of certain prominent futurists and an annotated guide to further reading.

Didsbury, Howard F., ed. *Student Handbook for The Study of the Future.* Washington, D.C.: World Future Society. 1979. 180 pages. Paperback. $5.95. This supplement to *The Study of the Future* is designed to help students develop a basic understanding of the field of futuristics. Much of the material has been "classroom-tested" by students in futures courses at Kean College of New Jersey.

Didsbury, Howard F., ed. *Instructor's Manual for The Study of the Future.* Washington, D.C.: World Future Society. 1979. 24 pages. Paperback. $2.00. A brief complementary volume to the *Student Handbook for The Study of the Future,* containing course outlines, research suggestions, teaching aids, bibliographical additions, and more.

Feather, Frank, ed. *Through the '80s: Thinking Globally, Acting Locally.* Washington, D.C.: World Future Society. 1980. 446 pages. Paperback. $12.50. Prepared in conjunction with the First Global Conference on the Future, held in Toronto, Canada, July 20-24, 1980. Subjects covered include the inventory of resources, economics, human values, communications, education, and health.

Jennings, Lane, and Sally Cornish, eds. *Education and the Future.* Washington, D.C.: World Future Society. 1980. 120 pages. Paperback. $4.95. Contains selections from THE FUTURIST and the *World Future Society Bulletin* on the future of education. Packed with ideas for the classroom.

Kierstead, Fred, Jim Bowman, and Christopher Dede, eds. *Educational Futures Sourcebook.* Washington, D.C.: World Future Society. 1979. 254 pages. Paperback. $5.95. This book contains selected papers from the first conference of the Education Section of the World Future Society, held in Houston, Texas, in October 1978.

Marien, Michael, ed. *Future Survey Annual 1980-81: A Guide to the Recent Literature of Trends, Forecasts, and Policy Proposals.* Washington, D.C.: World Future Society. 1981. 290 pages. Paperback. $25.00. Abstracts of about 1,500 books, reports, and articles divided into 15 sections: World Futures, International Economics, World Regions and Nations, Defense and Disarmament, Energy, Food and Agriculture, Environment and Resources, General Societal Directions, The Economy, Cities, Crime and Justice, Education, Health, Science and Technology, and Government. Future Survey Annual 1979 (255 pages, $25.00) is also still available.

Martin, Marie. *Films on the Future.* Washington, D.C.: World Future Society. 1977. 70 pages. Paperback. $3.00. This is the third revised and expanded version of the film guide first produced in 1971. The films are grouped by major subject areas (Education, Technology, etc.). A brief description of each film is supplemented by information about length, source, and rental costs.

Redd, Kathleen M., and Arthur M. Harkins, eds. *Education: A Time For Decisions.* Washington, D.C.: World Future Society. 1980. 301 pages. Paperback. $6.95. Selections from the Second Annual Conference of the Education Section of the World Future Society, arranged in four sections: Policies and Plans for the Present and the Future, Issues and Challenges for the Present and the Future, Theory and Visions for the Present and the Future, and Action and Examples for the Present and the Future.

THE STUDY OF THE FUTURE

An Introduction to the Art and Science of Understanding and Shaping Tomorrow's World

By Edward Cornish with members and staff of the World Future Society
World Future Society, Washington, D.C. 1977.
320 pages. Paperback. **Price: $9.50**

This exciting and unique volume is the Society's answer to the hundreds of inquiries it has received from people who want an easy-to-read, but authoritative and comprehensive introduction to futurism and future studies. The book includes:

- A concise history of futurism, from ancient times to today.
- A description of the philosophy of futurism.
- A discussion of the various scenarios developed by scholars for the future of our civilization.
- A detailed explanation of how organizations carry out futures research and how teachers give courses on the future.
- An annotated bibliography of selected books about the future.

—and much much more...

You'll meet the men and women whose contrasting viewpoints and informed perceptions have helped shape our visions of tomorrow's world—figures like Herman Kahn, Daniel Bell, John McHale, Alvin Toffler, Bertrand de Jouvenel, and Arthur C. Clarke.

You'll learn from non-technical summaries about the methods being used to make and test technological and social forecasts—methods such as Delphi studies, simulation gaming and computer model-building.

You'll examine how and why Big Business, Government, the Universities, and even Church and public service agencies are making future studies an essential part of their operations.

You'll discover ways to put futuristics to work for *you* in your own business, school and family environments.

We think you'll agree that *The Study of the Future* is a very special book. Here for the first time is a clear but authoritative introduction to the individuals, institutions and ideas at the cutting edge of humanity's never-ending exploration of the not-yet-known.

FUTURE SURVEY
pulls together fragments
of the future

Future Survey, the World Future Society's newest publication, pulls together fragments of the future in concise, jargon-free abstracts of books and articles on present trends and future possibilities.

Each monthly issue of *Future Survey* contains roughly 100 abstracts books from the lists of over 130 publishers, and articles selected from among the contents of some 150 English language magazines, newspapers, and journals.

The abstracts in *Future Survey* are grouped under general headings to encourage browsing, then cross-indexed by author and subject to aid quick reference. Specific subject headings vary from issue to issue, so that *Future Survey* can always bring you a broad sample of current opinion without imposing artificial distinctions to make available material fit into pre-conceived categories. Among the topics most often in *Future Survey* are: world futures, energy, environment and resources, Third World development, food and agriculture, the U.S. and global economies, cities, transportation, crime and justice, children, education, health, communications, science and technology, politics, and the future of future studies itself.

A one-year, 12-issue subscription to *Future Survey* costs $28 ($40 for libraries and institutions.) Our prediction is that you will be stimulated, forewarned, enlightened, ably assisted, and altogether pleased by *Future Survey*.

"We can't imagine any library, organization, government or business leader being without it."
New Magazine Review

".. indispensable ... for anyone seriously interested in the course of national and world affairs."
Victor Ferkiss (Georgetown University)

Order from:

**Book Service
World Future Society
4916 St. Elmo Avenue
Bethesda, Maryland
20814 U.S.A.**

WORLD FUTURE SOCIETY
An Association for the Study of Alternative Futures

The Society is an association of people interested in future social and technological developments. It is chartered as a non-profit scientific and educational organization in Washington, D.C., and is recognized as tax-exempt by the U.S. Internal Revenue Service. The World Future Society is independent, non-political and non-ideological.

The purpose of the World Future Society is to serve as an unbiased forum and clearinghouse for scientific and scholarly forecasts, investigations and intellectual explorations of the future. The Society's objectives, as stated in its charter, are as follows:

1. To contribute to a reasoned awareness of the future and the importance of its study, without advocating particular ideologies or engaging in political activities.
2. To advance responsible and serious investigation of the future.
3. To promote the development and improvement of methodologies for the study of the future.
4. To increase public understanding of future-oriented activities and studies.
5. To facilitate communication and cooperation among organizations and individuals interested in studying or planning for the future.

Membership is open to anyone seriously interested in the future. Since its founding in 1966, the Society has grown to more than 40,000 members in over 80 countries. Most members are U.S. residents, with growing numbers in Canada, Europe, Japan, and other countries. Members include many of the world's most distinguished scientists, scholars, business leaders, and government officials.

SOCIETY PROGRAMS

THE FUTURIST: A Journal of Forecasts, Trends, and Ideas About the Future.

This unique bimonthly journal reports the forecasts made by scientists and others concerning the coming years. It explores the possible consequences of these developments on the individual, institutions, and society, and discusses actions people may take to improve the future.

Books
The Society has published 11 books, including *The Study of the Future; The Future: A Guide to Information Sources; 1999: The World of Tomorrow; Through the '80s: Thinking Globally, Acting Lo-*

cally; *Educational Futures: Sourcebook I; Future Survey Annual 1 (1979); Education and the Future; Education: A Time for Decisions; Student Handbook for the Study of the Future;* and *Instructor's Manual for the Study of the Future.* Forthcoming are *The Information Society of Tomorrow* and *Future Survey Annual 2 (1980-81).*

Book Service
World Future Society members can purchase books, audio tapes, video tapes, films, games, and other future-oriented educational materials, often at substantial savings. The Society's unique "Future Bookstore" carries over 250 titles, and new releases are announced regularly in THE FUTURIST.

Tape Recordings
The Society stocks a variety of audio tapes, which are available at low cost to members. These cassettes, including

many popular sessions from the Society's Third General Assembly, cover science and technology, human values, government, education, environment, and many other subjects.

Chapter and Local Activities
The Society has over 100 local chapters, and more are forming. Chapters offer a variety of services and activities, including conferences, seminars, workshops, guest speakers, game nights, film screenings, and tours of local futuristic facilities. They provide opportunities for personal contacts with people interested in alternative futures.

Meetings
The Society sponsors periodic General Assemblies—large, interdisciplinary convocations—which allow members to interact with futurists on an international scale. The Third General Assembly, held in Toronto in July 1980, drew 5,400 participants from 45 countries. The Fourth General Assembly, whose theme is "Communications and the Future," will be held in Washington, D.C., in July 1982. The Society also sponsors specialized conferences, including annual conferences on education since 1978.